Action origami

over 25 animated paperfolding projects

rick beech

southwater

To Noelle and Nicholas with all my love and caring

Rick Beech: www.paper-magic.com

This edition is published by Southwater

Southwater is an imprint of Anness Publishing Limited
Hermes House, 88–89 Blackfriars Road, London SE1 8HA
tel. 020 7401 2077; fax 020 7633 9499; www.southwaterbooks.com; info@anness.com

© Anness Publishing Limited 2002

This edition distributed in the UK by The Manning Partnership Ltd
tel. 01225 478 444; fax 01225 478 440; sales@manning-partnership.co.uk

This edition distributed in the USA and Canada by National Book Network
tel. 301 459 3366; fax 301 459 1705; www.nbnbooks.com

This edition distributed in Australia by Pan Macmillan Australia
tel. 1300 135 113; fax 1300 135 103; email customer.service@macmillan.com.au

This edition distributed in New Zealand by The Five Mile Press (NZ) Ltd
tel. (09) 444 4144; fax (09) 444 4518; fivemilenz@clear.net.nz

A CIP catalogue record for this book is available from the British Library.

Publisher Joanna Lorenz
Managing Editor Judith Simons
Project Editor Louise Aikman
Photography John Freeman
Design Penny Dawes
Jacket Design Balley Design
Production Controller Clare Rae

Previously published as part of a larger compendium, *Origami*

1 3 5 7 9 10 8 6 4 2

contents

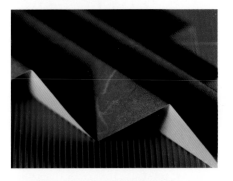

introduction

Welcome to this beautiful collection of action models and paper toys based upon the ancient Japanese art of Origami. In postwar England, many people were introduced to the art via the Rupert Bear annuals. The illustrator, Alfred Bestall, was a keen origamist and he often introduced the art into the Rupert stories. This colourful and enthralling book will also inspire enthusiasts. Beginning with simple traditional fare which have been produced by adults and children from both the East and West for many centuries, this enchanting collection moves through paper tricks and entertaining novelties using standard origami techniques, and concludes with more complex technical pieces guaranteed to provide you with a challenge. Paperfolding is a delightful and pleasurable experience to be enjoyed, so whether you are a complete beginner or an accomplished folder, there will be something here for you.

ABOVE Rupert Bear, folding an origami bird.

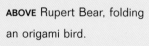

What is origami?

Origami is the Japanese art of paperfolding, the name deriving from two Japanese words, "ori" meaning to fold, and "kami" meaning paper. Dictionaries often suggest that it is the art in which bird forms and other models are folded from paper. From this brief description or from childhood memories, you may be forgiven for thinking that origami is limited to paper planes, waterbombs and fortune tellers. As you will soon discover, the interest in traditional origami folding continues, but the art has also advanced considerably in the last 30 to 40 years, so that a paper representation of virtually anything is now possible.

Origami is not limited to using only paper. Over the years, enthusiasts throughout the world have experimented with all kinds of materials while still adhering to the principles of folding. Lane Allen (USA), for example, has introduced Orikane. This entails folding models from several varieties of fine metal gauze. This material has two obvious differences from standard origami paper: it can be moulded and curved, which opens up a variety of creative possibilities. Another American, Jeremy Shafer, designed a pair of working Nail Clippers; after folding the model from a very fine Japanese foil paper, he went on to develop a version made out of similarly fine metal sheeting. David Brill (UK) surprised the folding community several years ago with his Ship in a Bottle, which required the bottle to be made of something transparent; he found the ideal

BELOW Miniature origami models on display at The Origami Gallery in Tokyo.

RIGHT A life-size Tyrannosaurus Rex skeleton folded from 21 sheets of paper and created by Issei Yoshino in 1996. Pictured at the 2nd International Origami Festival in Charlotte, North Carolina, USA.

material in the non-sticky acetate sheet book covering sold in many stationers. This material is also used by Mette Pederson (USA), who folds several unit modular pieces of origami (solid geometric forms made by joining many individual pieces of paper), which she then encases in a clear outer shell. The Dutch are particularly fond of Teabag Folding where they create two-dimensional mosaic patterns from ornate tea-bag wrappers, while dinner-napkin folding has always been popular around the world. There are many materials that are suitable for folding, and you can have great enjoyment adapting what you will learn in this book to the sources you can find in the world around you.

It is also a common misconception that the paper always has to be a square. There are hundreds of designs using various rectangles, different regular polyhedra and even circles. Nor are you limited to the number of sheets of paper used for each design.

What isn't origami?

Unlike other paper arts, origami is highly disciplined, in that only the paper folds create the subject. Indeed, purists will frown upon the mere mention of the words "cut" or "stick", and are unlikely to agree that the odd slit here and there to help make a fold possible is true origami. So, designing origami can be a complex procedure, as you try to realize your idea while taking account of the restrictions imposed by the medium.

Action origami

Both historically and in more contemporary origami circles perhaps one of the greatest challenges is to design a model which, within the constraining properties of the paper, yields some kind of mechanism whereby action and movement are introduced. This book helps you to discover the fascinating techniques behind this phenomenon.

Many of the world's leading paper artists and origami experts began paperfolding as children, experimenting with basic designs, such as airplanes to see if they could improve upon them. From these simple ideas, more complex techniques were discovered. Using scrap items such as old train tickets, many ideas were created. For example, "frogs" were produced that actually jumped like the real thing. The traditional "banger" and "flapping bird" are also essential playground folds that have been collected and taught from generation to generation. All are illustrated and described here, along with many other superb animated designs to capture your imagination.

Paper,
Techniques
& Base Folds

Before you begin folding the models that appear in

this book, it is essential that you first become

familiar with the properties of certain papers and

recognize the importance of folding accurately.

You will also need to acquire a firm grasp of simple

procedures and some more complex moves, such as

inside reverse folds, rabbit ears and sinks.

Once committed to memory, these specialized

techniques will give you the skills you need to

produce absolutely anything, at any level,

in origami.

paper

Although most origami models can be folded from almost any type of paper, there are certain designs that beg for the use of specialist material, whether purely for aesthetic beauty, or because of the weight and thickness of the chosen medium. A wide variety of interesting and unusual papers can now be purchased from gift shops, stationers and specialist shops alike, or even found around the home. Enjoy experimenting with different types of paper.

Duo paper

Paper with a different colour on the reverse side is a great asset to origami enthusiasts, as it helps provide areas of alternate colour to finished models. Available in pre-cut specialist packs, you can now find such paper in standard-size packs and even in rolls. Look out for paper that is described as 'fadeless duo' and is sold as art material.

Specialist origami paper

Pre-cut packs of multi-coloured origami paper, available in a wide variety of sizes, colours and patterns, are not that easy to find locally. Thankfully, origami societies around the world have an excellent mailing service supplying different types and sizes of paper, as do a number of specialist suppliers. This kind of paper is fairly flimsy, yet will crease well, so it is ideal for practising your models, although you may prefer to use a different material once you have mastered a particular design.

Textured paper

As well as patterned paper, there are also many different kinds of paper available that have a texture to the surface. This proves particularly useful when folding animals and other living creatures, as it enhances the realism of the subject. Such papers as elephant hide, Ingres and watercolour can also be ideal wet folding mediums.

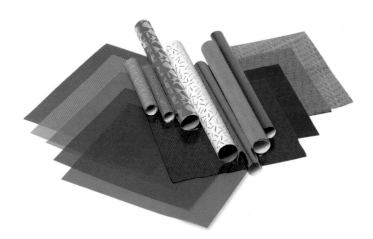

Metallic, foil, opaque & shiny papers

These are some of the more difficult materials to work with, but if you persevere the results can look spectacular. Paper-backed foil is widely available, and this material has the property of being able to be curved and moulded. Care must be taken, however, as some foil papers, thin plastic materials and opaque paper can be quite difficult to crease well, and reversed creases can crack, whiten or even split.

Washi & other handmade paper

In specialist paper shops you can buy Japanese washi paper, which is a soft, fibred material. This and other handmade papers from around the world give lighter creases to your folding and a softer, less angular look to final models.

Patterned paper

Gift wrap can be wonderful paper to fold with, as it is often quite sturdy (medium weight) and nowadays there is so much choice around. Look out for musical manuscript, swirling watermark-patterned paper, wood grain appearance and abstract gold, black and silver colourings in gift shops and the larger department stores.

Materials from around the home

Before you go searching for special or expensive paper to fold with, remember that your home may be already a great source of folding material. Copy paper, napkins, spare wallpaper, index cards, bank notes (those foreign currencies saved from holiday expeditions), and even magazines or newspapers can be used to make interesting and practical origami models.

equipment and preparation

There are very few essential origami tools to purchase, or preparation techniques to learn. However, it is worth familiarizing yourself with tools you might need, many of which, such as scissors and rulers, are household items, and making sure that they are within reach before you begin folding.

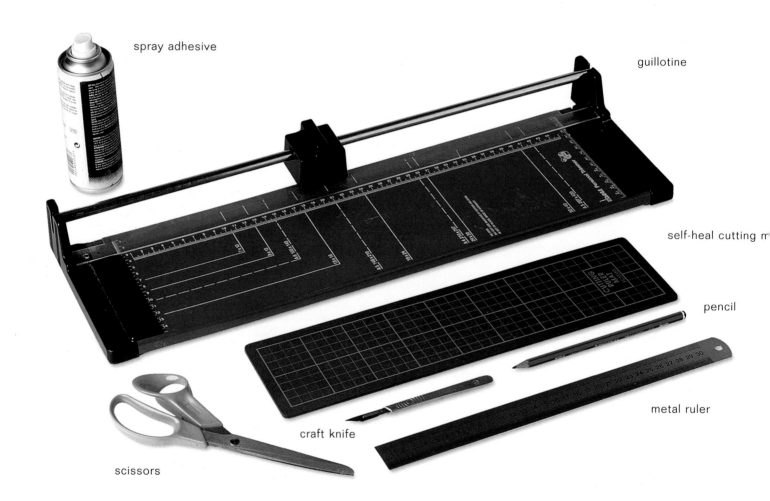

spray adhesive

guillotine

self-heal cutting m

pencil

metal ruler

craft knife

scissors

Equipment

Although plenty of origami models can be made with nothing more than a piece of paper and a pair of hands, there are a few pieces of equipment that are essential to a dedicated origamist. Spray adhesive is useful for sticking two sheets of different-coloured or textured paper together, but always follow the safety instructions. A guillotine is a worthwhile investment if you are practising origami on a regular basis. They come in a variety of sizes and a range of prices and have the advantage of cutting a very straight edge. A cutting knife is a very useful tool as its extremely sharp blade makes cutting through any thickness of paper simple. Always use a metal ruler when working with a craft knife and rest the paper on a self-healing cutting mat. This will not only protect the work surface, but will also prevent slipping and thus accidental cuts, as well as extending the life of the blade. A sturdy pair of paper scissors can often be just as effective as any other cutting tool, but make sure that you draw a faint, accurate pencil line on the paper before you start to cut.

Using a guillotine

Often you will require a specific size of paper, and a guillotine is a great help here, particularly as you can align your paper with the straight measured edge to ensure that you make a cut that is at right angles to the straight edge. It is possible to cut two or three sheets at a time, but you will get a cleaner cut if you only cut one sheet at a time.

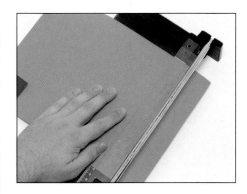

1 Place one edge of the paper flush with the ruled edge of the guillotine.

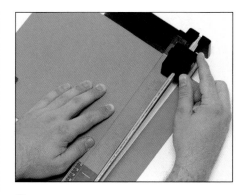

2 Holding the paper in place with one hand, use your other hand to slide the cutting blade across it, making a clean accurate cut.

Spray mounting

Spray mounting two sheets of paper together, back to back, is a useful technique for thickening an existing outer paper for a certain project, or for providing a chosen combination of colours. Spray mounting foil paper to tissue paper yields a material that can be shaped and moulded, curved and sculptured more easily than conventional paper, while the tissue paper gives a more realistic look to living creatures.

2 Carefully place the reverse side of the second sheet (the side you do not wish to be visible) on top of the upturned sticky first sheet. The second sheet should ideally be slightly smaller than the first, so that a thin border will appear around the edges of this second sheet.

4 With a craft knife and ruler, or with a guillotine, trim off the excess paper around the edges.

SAFETY

As with all aerosols, it is important to read the instructions on the spray adhesive can and follow them closely. If possible, use the spray outside and wear a mask. Otherwise, make sure that you are in a well-ventilated area and that you have protected the surfaces around you. Newspaper and cardboard offer cheap and effective protection.

1 Protect your worksurface with newspaper. Select two sheets of paper, and lay one face down on your spraying surface. Using spray adhesive, spray a fine mist evenly across the paper.

3 Carefully smooth out any wrinkles or creases in the back-coated layers by running your hand over the upper surface, pressing firmly as you go.

techniques and tips

Although you are probably keen to get started on the projects, read this section first so that you understand the standard techniques and basic procedures before you make a model. Learning how to fold your paper correctly, and familiarizing yourself with the photograph step instructions are key stages to successful models. The more you practise folding the basic techniques the more you will enjoy making origami.

How to fold

The first golden rule is to have something smooth and flat to use as your folding surface, preferably of a larger area than the sheet of paper that you are going to fold. The second is to make all the creases in the paper, by folding in a direction away from you, taking the edge or corner nearest to you and folding bottom to top. This is simply to make the folding easier, and to give you more control over the paper than if you tried to bring the upper edge or corner towards you or by folding side to side.

Wherever possible, the photographs will follow a natural folding sequence so that you will not need to alter the position or orientation of the paper in order to fold away from you. Always make firm, sharp creases. The neater and sharper you make the creases, the better the finished model will appear. Do not hurry to finish the model. Relax, take care and enjoy what you are folding. Do not be discouraged if your first attempt ends in disappointment, because you have not been able to complete the model. If it is not as well folded as the illustration suggests, just try again.

Ways to fold

Technically, there are only two actual ways to fold: either a valley fold, where a corner, edge or flap will remain to the front and in sight; or a mountain fold, taking a portion of the paper behind the rest of the model and out of sight. All other folds are variations of the valley and mountain folds.

Valley fold

1 Fold the lower edge of the paper upward, to an arbitrary point. Hold the fold in place with one hand, and smooth out the crease with the other hand.

2 This is a valley (or forward) fold.

Mountain fold

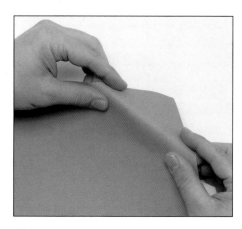

1 With fingers and thumbs at the ends of the crease you intend to make, fold the paper behind, pinching in the fold. Here, the fold is made to a corner.

2 Smooth out the crease. This is a mountain (or backward) fold.

Pre-crease

Often you will fold and unfold the paper in order to leave a crease which will act as a guideline for a later definite fold. This is called a pre-crease.

Pinch crease

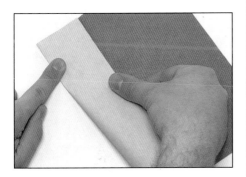

1 Sometimes when you are making a crease, you do not actually want to crease through every layer of paper, or even all the way across the paper, but wish to make a tiny mark or short crease line to act as a guide for a later definite fold. To do this, simply apply pressure to a part of the fold.

2 Unfold, leaving a small crease mark as your guide.

Dividing into thirds

Often you will need to be able to fold the paper accurately into three equal parts or thirds. This procedure is a little experimental, so take your time and fold carefully.

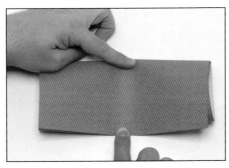

1 Using a rectangular sheet of paper, and with the shorter sides horizontal, fold the lower edge upward, to a point which you judge to be one-third of the way down from the upper edge. Make a very soft crease.

2 Fold the upper edge down over the section of paper folded in step 1. Make a soft crease. Unfold the paper. If you have estimated the flap in step 1 correctly, you should now have three horizontal borders of equal depth. Each outer raw edge could then be folded inward, and would meet with one of the creases made in steps 1–2. If you are slightly out in your estimation, then try again, making the initial crease slightly higher or lower than before.

Pleat fold

This is the concertina effect produced when a flap is doubled back on itself.

1 Make two parallel valley folds in a sheet of paper. Turn the paper over so that these horizontal creases are now mountain creases.

2 Pinch the lower crease between fingers and thumb of each hand. Slide this crease and the paper beneath away from you, until you can lie it upon the upper crease. Flatten the model.

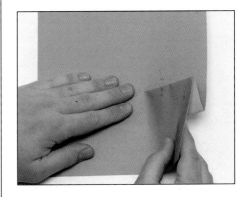

ABOVE The completed pleat fold.

Special moves

There are several special moves in origami, standard techniques that are used in countless models in one form or another. Once you have learned these basic routines you will always be able to adapt your skill and knowledge to whichever project you are tackling.

Inside reverse fold

This is one of the most common procedures, which occurs in two basic forms: tucking a flap inside the model or changing the angle of a point.

Tucking a flap inside

1 Fold a rectangular sheet of paper in half and rotate the paper 180° so that the fold you have just made now runs horizontally across the top.

2 Fold the vertical side at the right down so that it lies along the lower edge.

3 Unfold step 2.

4 By slightly opening out the fold made in step 1 you will see that the crease made in step 2 runs through both sides of the paper. One of the creases will appear as a valley fold, the other as a mountain fold. Both need to be mountain folds, so pinch the valley fold into a mountain fold.

5 Pushing inwards on the spine crease that originally ran along the upper edge of the right-hand portion of the paper, allow the triangular flap to be turned inside out, as it is pushed between the outer layers of the paper.

6 Allow the two outer corners to come back together as you flatten the paper.

ABOVE The completed inside reverse fold.

Folding a point

1 Fold a piece of paper into a Kite base (see p.22), then fold in half lengthways along the centre crease.

2 Make an arbitrary valley fold as shown, bringing the point downwards, and changing the angle of the point.

3 Unfold step 2.

4 Slightly open out the two lower sloping edges at the right, that run to the point, and see how the crease made in step 2 passes through both layers of the paper, front and back. Once again, make both creases forming the V shape mountain folds (change the direction of the valley fold to a mountain fold), as you begin to push down on the spine crease running along the upper right edge.

5 Allow the paper to turn inside out, as the spine crease of the point bends backwards on itself and is pushed down between the two outer layers.

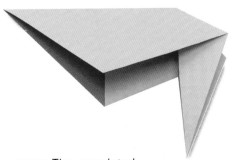

ABOVE The completed inside reverse fold.

Outside reverse fold

This move is similar to the inside reverse fold, except that the layers of paper are wrapped around the outside in order to effect the angle change.

1 Prepare the point by folding a Kite base (see p.22), then fold this in half lengthways using the centre crease.

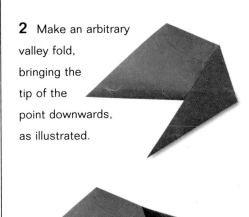

2 Make an arbitrary valley fold, bringing the tip of the point downwards, as illustrated.

3 Unfold step 2.

4 Open out the two upper edges leading to the tip of the point. As with the inside reverse fold, the crease made in step 2 now passes through both layers of paper, front and back.

5 Using the existing V shape of creases, turn the point outside on itself. The spine crease leading to the tip of the point is changed in direction from a valley fold to a mountain fold.

6 Allow the front and rear layers to come back together as you flatten the paper.

ABOVE The completed outside reverse fold.

Rabbit ear

This is where two adjacent edges are folded in simultaneously. As the two edges come together, they are squashed to form another point.

1 Fold a square of paper in half from corner to corner. Unfold.

2 Rotate the paper around so that the crease made in step 1 is now vertical to you, then fold the paper in half once more, corner to corner, making a second crease perpendicular to the first. Unfold.

3 Fold the lower left sloping edge upward to lie along the horizontal centre crease.

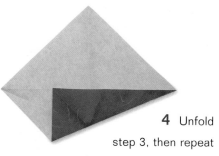

4 Unfold step 3, then repeat step 3 using the lower right sloping edge.

5 Unfold step 4. Simultaneously refold the lower sloping edges as folded in steps 3–4, to the centre crease.

6 Squeeze the corner nearest to you to a point, using the vertical diagonal crease. The new point will project upwards at right angles to the rest of the model.

RIGHT The completed rabbit ear.

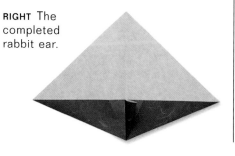

Squash fold

This is where a flap is squashed down into a new position.

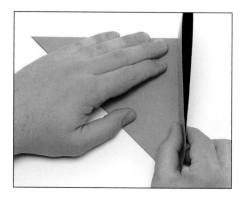

1 Fold a square of paper in half diagonally, then in half again. Unfold the second stage and arrange so that the folded edge runs along the top. Raise the right-hand flap of the model upward on the vertical centre crease, so that it is at right angles to the folding surface.

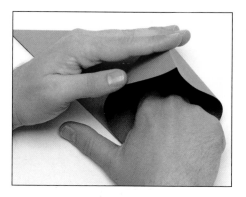

2 Separate the two layers of the raised flap with one hand, and with your other hand squash the paper flat, bringing the spine crease of the raised flap down to lie along the vertical crease.

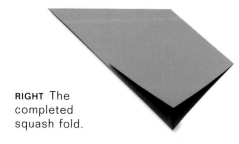

RIGHT The completed squash fold.

Crimp fold

This is a useful move for adding a 3D effect or sculptured look to models.

1 Fold a rectangular sheet of paper in half, bringing the shorter sides together. Rotate the paper around so that the shorter sides are now horizontal. Make an arbitrary valley fold in the paper, at about the halfway mark, but at an angle, so that the portion of paper that you are folding comes to rest offset to the left.

2 Fold the upper flap back downwards on itself, making another valley crease. At the right as you look, this crease begins at the same place as the crease made in step 1, so that when you pull the paper back downward, you do so as far as you can comfortably go.

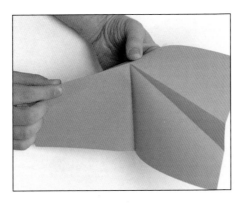

3 Open out all the creases. You will now see that the two creases you made in steps 1–2 pass through both layers of the paper, front and back. Whether you want to make an inside or an outside crimp (see final pictures), you need to adopt the same principle as with the inside and outside reverse folds: on one side of the model the valley and mountain creases are in the opposite direction to the same creases on the other side of the paper. Opposite pairs of the same crease need to be either both valley folds, or mountain folds. You will, therefore, need to change the direction manually of both creases on one side of the paper.

4 Step 5 completed, seen from above, showing the principal crease from step 1 restored. Take hold of the paper with each hand, at opposite ends of this folded edge.

5 Holding the left side of the paper firmly in place, allow the right hand to bring the right portion of the paper downwards. The creases made in steps 1–2 will now allow the paper to flatten into the position shown. Both sides of the paper will appear identical. This is an outside crimp, where the crease furthest to the right is a mountain fold.

ABOVE The completed outside crimp fold.

ABOVE If the crease furthest to the right is a valley crease, then the result will be as shown. The completed inside crimp fold.

Swivel fold

Fairly lengthy preparation is needed in order to be able to illustrate and practise this origami move.

1 Fold the paper in half, corner to opposite corner, to pre-crease the diagonal. Unfold and arrange as a square. Fold the lower left corner and lower edge upward to lie along the diagonal crease line.

2 Fold the lower right corner directly upwards by an arbitrary amount.

3 Unfold step 2. Fold the left-hand edge across making a vertical crease perpendicular to the upper edge. This crease should meet with the crease made in step 2.

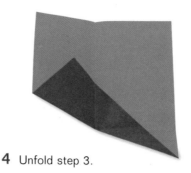

4 Unfold step 3.

5 Now, keeping the triangular flap folded in step 1 in place, refold the crease from step 2 in the underside layer only, which will cause the paper of the upper layer at the right-hand side to lift up, and not to lie flat.

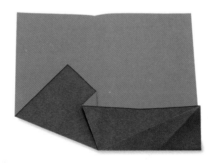

6 The paper should naturally "crimp" across to the left, where the vertical valley crease in the upper layer of the paper pulls the excess material with it. The central area of paper then seems to "swivel" into place. Flatten the model. The completed swivel fold.

Sink fold

This move entails a closed point to be sunk inside the model. You may need to practise this move several times before you perfect it.

1 Prepare a Waterbomb base (see pp.24–5).

2 Fold the top corner down by an arbitrary amount.

3 Unfold step 2, then open the Waterbomb base out slightly, and look at the model from above.

4 In the centre of the paper you will locate a small square, which was created by the crease made in step 2, passing through all the layers of the paper. Pinch-crease all these creases as mountain folds. Some are mountain folds already.

5 Pushing this central square inwards on existing creases, carefully collapse the Waterbomb base once again.

6 Flatten the paper, ensuring that there are two flaps to the left and two flaps to the right of the Waterbomb base. What was the central square has now become inverted into the model. The completed sink fold.

Wet folding

Making origami with damp paper allows you to mould and shape the model to a greater degree than you can with dry paper. Start off with a simple model that you have folded many times before, one without pointed corners and sharp creases. The larger the square you start with, the thicker the paper you can use.

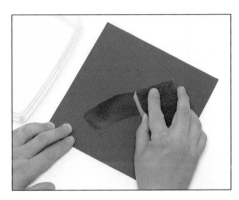

1 To dampen the paper, use a damp sponge or absorbent cloth and carefully brush both sides of the paper until the sheet is uniformly damp. The key word is damp; not wet. Only experience can really tell you how damp the paper needs to be, but if it becomes shiny, allow it to dry slightly before proceeding.

2 Once a crease has been made, you can use the warmth of your fingers to partially dry out that area so it will retain its shape.

3 Continue to crease the paper while moulding the folds as required. Master-folder Robert Lang recommends using masking tape to help reinforce weak areas of the paper (such as where several creases meet). The tape can be removed when the paper is dry.

4 Since the aim of wet folding is "animation" of the fold, you should encourage three-dimensionality wherever possible and keep non-essential creases to a minimum. A consequence is that most of your folding will have to be performed in the air.

5 The feel and appearance of wet-folded origami is impossible to match in any other way.

base folds

Throughout ancient Japanese origami tradition, as well as by contemporary experimentation, certain basic folds, or bases, have evolved. These are standard and easily recognizable starting points from which hundreds of different models derive. It is worth committing these to memory along with the miscellaneous tips and techniques from the preceding pages. Allow them to become familiar, enjoy folding them, and try to understand the crease patterns and formations of each of them, as they will appear in so many wonderful designs. Almost anyone can do origami, as long as they take the utmost care in following the instructions. Do not assume anything, but look closely at each photograph and text caption, until you clearly understand what you are required to do. With time and practice, you will be able to fold many of the models in this book without reading the text.

ABOVE Buttonhole flower made using the Kite base and Waterbomb base.

Kite base

1 Begin by folding a square of paper in half diagonally, bringing together two opposite corners. Unfold the paper and rotate it so that the crease you have just made is vertical to you, that is it runs from the upper corner to the lower corner, when the paper is arranged as a diamond, as shown.

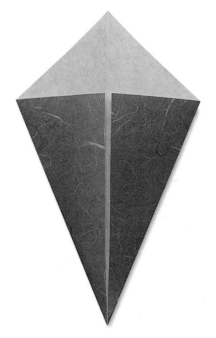

2 Fold each of the lower sloping outer edges inward to lie along the vertical crease line made in step 1. The completed Kite base.

Blintz fold

Deriving from a Yiddish word of
Ukrainian origin, a blintz is literally a
thin pancake folded to contain a
cheese or other filling. Because a
blintz is folded with all the outer
corners to the centre, the name was
taken by Gershon Legman and other
1950s paperfolders to refer to the act
of folding all the four corners of the
square of paper to the centre. There
are two principal methods to achieve
this, both shown here. The second
method is best when teaching origami
to children and to the blind and
partially-sighted, for it is far simpler
to aim for a folded edge than to try to
bring the four outer corners to a point
within the area of paper.

method 1

1 Fold a square of paper in half
diagonally, bringing together opposite
corners. Unfold, rotate the paper so that
the crease you have just made is now
vertical to you (it runs from the upper
corner to the lower corner), then fold in
half again, bottom to top. This will add a
pre-crease perpendicular to the first
crease you made. Unfold once more.

2 Carefully fold each of the four outer
corners in turn to the centre, that is
where the two diagonal creases you
made in step 1 intersect. There should
be no overlap with any of the new
corners formed, and all the raw edges
should run evenly side by side to the
centre. The completed Blintz fold.

method 2

1 Begin with the predominant
colour face upwards. Arrange the
paper on your folding surface so
that it appears as a square, in
other words, with horizontal and
vertical sides. Fold the lower edge
up to the upper edge, then rotate
the paper 180° so that the fold
you made in step 1 now runs
horizontally along the upper edge.

2 Fold the lower outer corners, single
layer only, upward, so that what were
the vertical raw edges now lie along the
upper horizontal edge.

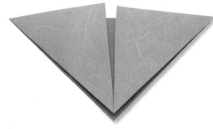

3 Turn the paper over and repeat step
2 on this side of the paper.

4 Take hold of the two independent
corners at the right angle of the
triangular form created in step 3, and
pull apart.

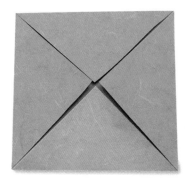

5 Lay the paper flat on your folding
surface, with the blintzed flaps on top.
The completed Blinz fold.

Fish base

1 Begin by folding the Kite base.

2 Turn the paper over, keeping the sharper of the two points at either end of the diagonal fold at the bottom.

3 Fold the lower sharp point up to the top, folding the model in half.

4 Turn the paper over, keeping it arranged the same way.

5 At the lower half of the model, you have two independent flaps. Holding down the right-hand half of the model flat to your folding surface, take hold of the loose outer corner of the flap on the left side, and pull it towards you, allowing the pocket behind to open up. As you do this, carefully begin squashing the outer left-hand edge inward, lining up the new creases that you are making with both the upper corner and the corner you have just pulled down and repositioned.

6 Step 5 completed.

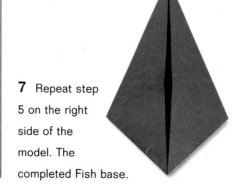

7 Repeat step 5 on the right side of the model. The completed Fish base.

Waterbomb base

1 Fold a square of paper in half, bringing opposite corners together. Unfold, then rotate the paper so that the first crease is vertical to you. Fold in half corner to corner once more, adding a pre-crease that is perpendicular to the first crease. Unfold once more.

2 Turn the paper over, and make a further pre-crease, folding the paper in half side to side, then unfold and turn back over to the original side. The diagonal creases will appear as valleys, while the remaining crease, which needs to be arranged horizontally across the paper, is a mountain.

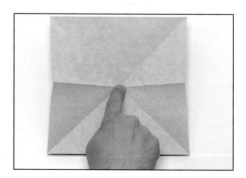

3 With one finger, push down on the paper at the centre. The creases in the paper will flex gently, and the centre will show indications of becoming concave.

4 Take hold of the paper between fingers and thumbs of either hand along the vertical side edges, at a point just below the horizontal crease made in step 2.

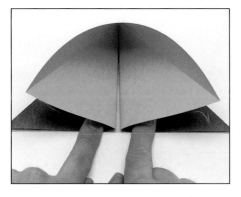

5 Using the existing lower-diagonal creases, carefully bring the two sides in to meet, the sides flattening down to lie upon the central triangular area at the lower half of the paper.

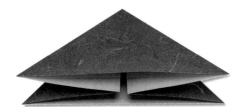

6 Squash the upper layer of the paper flat, so that all the creases collapse into position, forming a pyramid. The completed Waterbomb base.

Preliminary base

1 Using a square of paper with the predominant colour face up, fold the paper in half, bringing opposite corners together. Unfold the paper then fold the paper in half again, bringing the remaining two corners together. Unfold again, and turn the paper over.

2 Now fold the paper in half side to side in both directions, each time folding the outer edges together and unfolding. The principle is the same as when folding the pre-creases in step 1.

3 Refold one of the creases made in step 2. Then take hold of the paper between fingers and thumbs of either hand, placed about halfway across each side of the paper, as shown.

4 In an upward circular motion, bring all your fingers and thumbs together simultaneously, causing all the four outer corners of the paper to meet at the top.

5 Flatten the model. This is achieved by swinging the large flap projecting upward down to one side, whilst swivelling the flap underneath the model across to the other side. There should now be two flaps pointing to the left, and two pointing to the right.

ABOVE The completed Preliminary base.

Bird base

1 Fold a Preliminary base, and begin by arranging the paper so that the open end, where the raw edges and corners meet, lies pointing toward you. Fold the lower sloping edges of the upper layer of the paper inward to lie along the vertical centre crease.

2 Fold the upper corner (the closed point) down over the flaps folded in step 1. Make a firm crease.

3 Unfold steps 1–2, so that you are back with the Preliminary base.

4 Using the crease made in step 2, lift up the single layer of paper at the lower corner, and raise it upward. The paper opens out, and this corner now comes to lie upon your folding surface.

5 Now allow the sides to be squashed inward to meet the vertical centre line. Steps 4–5 are often referred to as a petal fold.

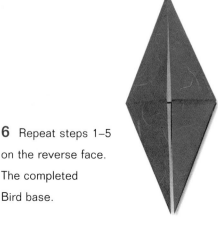

6 Repeat steps 1–5 on the reverse face. The completed Bird base.

Frog Base

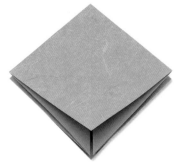

1 Begin with a Preliminary base, and arrange so that the open end, where the raw edges and corners meet, lies pointing toward you.

2 Using the vertical centre crease as an axis by which all the large triangular flaps can be rotated, lift up one flap at the right, so that it projects outward at right angles to the rest of the model.

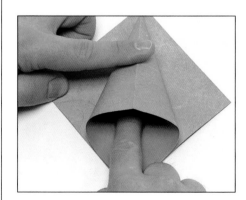

3 Separating the two layers of this flap, place one finger inside the pocket, and allow the paper to open and hollow out. With your other hand, squash the paper down, allowing the spine crease along the upper edge of this flap to come to rest along the centre line.

4 Step 3 completed.

5 You now have an upper section of paper resembling a kite shape. Using the vertical axis once again, fold the right half of this kite shape to the left.

6 You can now raise a second large flap from the right, and repeat steps 3–4. Repeat steps 3–4 in the same way with the remaining two large flaps, rotating the layers as you proceed.

7 With the squash folds from step 6 showing on the upper surface, fold the lower raw edges either side inward to lie along the vertical centre crease.

8 Unfold step 7.

9 We are now going to perform a petal fold similar to that of the Bird base. Carefully lift up the raw edge which cuts across the paper, connecting left and right outer corners of the model. Taking the single layer only, fold this edge upwards, making a valley crease horizontally across the paper, joining the upper extremes of the creases made in step 7. You will need to pinch this crease in manually. Allow the two outer edges to squash inward to the centre line.

10 Carefully manipulate the paper so that this petal fold lines up evenly with the vertical centre line, where the new point should rest.

11 Step 10 completed on one flap. Repeat steps 7–10 on the three similar faces, rotating the layers around the central vertical axis to accomplish this.

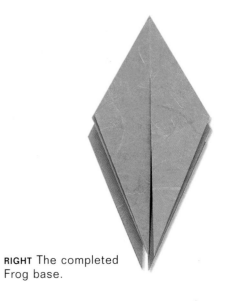

RIGHT The completed Frog base.

The Projects

Working origami is ingeniously clever, as are the origamists who devised the many and varied mechanisms for making the hundreds of models that flap, fly, spin, "talk", make a noise or have some kind of movement. There are some very simple pieces, which children will delight in, and others that take more skill and time, but which make for a climactic end to the folding sequence.

jumping frog

Underground tickets, index cards, rail tickets and other fairly stiff material needs to be used for this model, so that you create tension and a spring in the hind legs, which you would not have if folding with conventional paper. The proportions of the rectangle used aren't too critical, neither is the colour, although green is a fairly obvious choice. A 13 x 7.5cm/5 x 3in index card works particularly well.

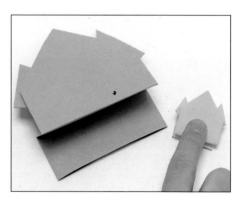

1 Position the rectangle with the shorter edges horizontal. At the top end of the rectangle, form a Waterbomb base.

2 Fold each of the sharp points upward and outward, each crease beginning from the centre line, but so that there is a gap between the head and each of the front legs when the step is completed.

3 Fold the vertical outer edges in to lie along the centre line. This will align with the point where the legs join.

4 Fold the lower edge upward as far as it will go comfortably (with stiff card this is as far as the inner layers will allow).

5 Fold the upper edge back down towards you, to the lower folded edge, creating a pleat in the material, which will be the springy hind legs.

6 The completed Jumping Frog. Make him jump by placing your index finger on his back, pressing down as you then "stroke" the card to the rear of the model. You will be surprised at how far the frog will spring.

glider

Paper planes have always been popular and there are hundreds of designs. This simple glider, which is launched with a fairly graceful throw, is a variation using classic ideas. Use fairly sturdy paper; A5 (14.5 x 21cm/5¾ x 8¼in) being an ideal size.

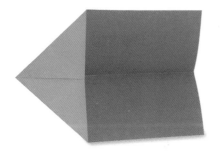

1 Fold the rectangular paper in half, bringing the two longest sides together. This establishes the centre crease. Fold two corners at one end of the model inward to lie along this crease.

2 Turn the paper over and rotate through 90°. The outline of the model now comprises a rectangle at the top and a triangle at the bottom. Fold the lower point up so that the triangle comes to rest on top of the rectangle, the crease running along the edges of the flaps folded in step 1.

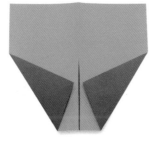

3 Noting the distance of the height of the triangle, determine a point in your mind approximately one-third of the way down from the top point. Then fold in the lower corners to meet at the intersection of this point and the vertical centre crease. (The nose of the glider will not be sharply pointed, as in many conventional models.)

4 To lock the two flaps folded in step 3 into place, fold the point of the inner triangle towards you, over the top of these flaps. Do not force this point to fold further than it will naturally go, or you will tear the edges of the two side flaps.

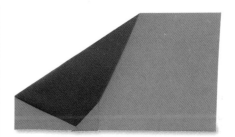

5 Mountain fold the model in half along the centre crease, so that all the flaps and folds are on the outside. Rotate to the position shown.

6 Fold the sloping edge along the top of the model down (single layer only) so that it lies along the lower horizontal edge. Repeat on the reverse, then open out the wings slightly before launching. From the rear, the glider should appear more like a letter Y than a letter T, with the wings raised up slightly. Hold the small triangular flap underneath the glider between thumb and finger, then launch with a forward and upward throw.

banger

This simple design is one of the few that
the author has regularly taught whilst doing guest
slots on radio broadcasts. Try teaching someone by verbal
instruction only, and see if they can complete the model. Also try
folding it from different materials and compare the results in terms of the
noise made. You can use newspaper, glossy magazine or parcel paper to good effect.
Warning: be sure to stand clear of your folding surface when working the banger, to avoid
bruised knuckles.

1 Fold a rectangle (A3 [29 x 42cm/11½
x 16½in], minimum) in half, bringing the
long edges together. Unfold, then fold all
four corners inward to lie along the
crease just made.

2 Fold the model in half, bottom to top.

3 Fold in half again,
bringing the sharp
points together.

4 Upper layer only, fold the lower
edge back on a diagonal crease
to lie along the folded edge
created in step 3.

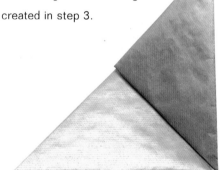

5 Repeat on the reverse face.

HOW TO USE

Hold the banger tightly by the corner that has the two independent sharp points.
Make sure that the longest side faces toward you. Hold high in the air, as shown,
then bring the whole model down sharply, as if cracking a whip. The inner flap
shoots out, producing a loud "bang". To reload, simply refold the banger.

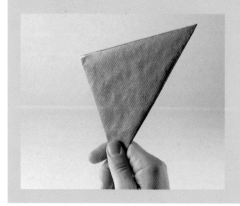

stackers

This model was designed by Michael LaFosse, and executed with amazing aplomb when he visited a convention in England organized by the British Origami Society. Try folding from standard origami paper (15cm/6in square), as it is quite thin it works well with this model. You can fold any number of stacker units, but four is recommended to start with.

1 Fold a square of thin, crisp paper in half diagonally. Pinch-mark the centre of the lower edge, then fold the single layer at the top down to the bottom.

4 Using the mountain creases created in step 2, fold each of the sharp points backwards, and tuck in the pocket (behind the horizontal folded edge underneath).

7 Fold the lower point up to meet the folded edge, one layer only. Repeat on the reverse side. The stacker should now appear "corrugated".

2 Fold each of the sharp points inward to meet with the large triangular flap.

3 Unfold step 2. Fold the sharp points up to the top. The right side is shown completed. Repeat with the left side.

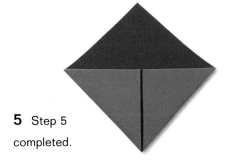

5 Step 5 completed.

6 Using the vertical centre crease, mountain fold the model in half and turn the model around, as shown.

HOW TO USE

Make at least three more units, then stack them on top of each other and lay them in the palm of your hand, with the two-coloured side uppermost. The thicker, heavier end should face towards your fingertips and all the units should face the same way. Throw the pile of stackers high into the air. They will separate and fly off in different directions.

barking dog

This design is by Ulrike Krallmann-Wenzel. How clever to be able to add a couple of creases to what is a standard base, open out the paper completely, re-collapse it, and have a wonderful action toy. Begin with a square of crisp paper, preferably duo.

1 Fold a Preliminary base, with the opening facing you. Fold in both layers on the left-hand side so that they rest at a point a little below the centre.

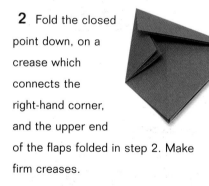

2 Fold the closed point down, on a crease which connects the right-hand corner, and the upper end of the flaps folded in step 2. Make firm creases.

3 Open the paper out enough to be able to see the crease pattern formed. Using the photograph as a guide, change the direction of certain creases, so that you can collapse the paper into the form shown. See how particular creases on either side of the model need to be made to face the same direction.

4 Steps 3 and 4 completed.

5 Turn the tip of the nose outside on itself, which makes use of the reverse colour of your paper.

HOW TO USE

To make the dog "bark", hold him by the chest with one hand, the tail with the other (you will need to supply the noise yourself). Gently pull the tail, allowing the paper to open and collapse back. The head will raise in excitement.

zoomerang

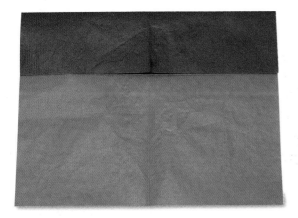

Sanny Ang, an Australian paperfolder, visited England a while back, and amazed crowds by demonstrating how to throw this model away from you in such a way, that it can be "trained" to land on your head on its way back. Use a square of thin, crisp paper for best results, and practise adjusting the proportions of the model's folds to give the effect you desire.

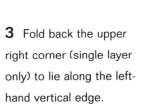

1 After pre-creasing the horizontal and vertical halfway lines of a square of paper, fold the upper edge down to the centre.

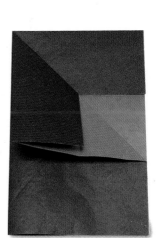

3 Fold back the upper right corner (single layer only) to lie along the left-hand vertical edge.

2 Valley fold the model in half side to side, left to right.

4 Repeat step 3 on the reverse face. Then open up the model from below, swinging the larger flap in between layers upward, so that it rests perpendicular to your folding surface. The side flaps should arrange themselves as shown.

▶

5 Open out and separate the layers of this 90° section, and make a squash fold, bringing the folded edge down to the baseline, forming a large triangle. Turn the model over.

6 Step 5 completed.

7 Fold down the upper corner so that if you were to imagine a line drawn horizontally across the reverse-coloured central diamond, the tip of the corner would meet this line.

8 Fold the same corner back up on itself.

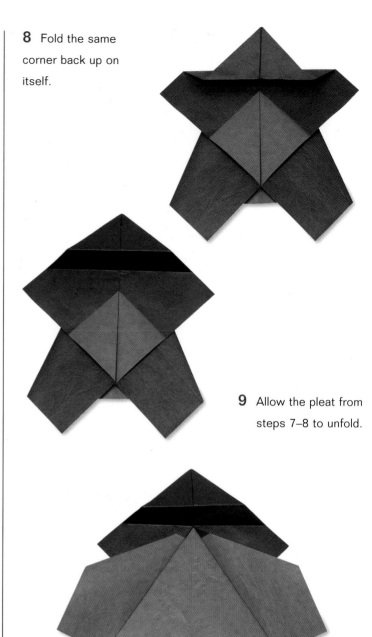

9 Allow the pleat from steps 7–8 to unfold.

10 Fold out the lower flaps, on creases connecting the lower extreme right and left corners with the vertical centre line, where it intersects with the crease made in step 7. Sharply pre-crease, then unfold the flaps.

11 Reform the pleat from steps 7–8. Mountain fold the model in half along the centre crease.

12 Rotating the paper around slightly, and folding one layer only at a time, fold the wing section across the model. The crease begins at the corner of the pleat, and brings the outer edge of the wing approximately to the mountain-folded edge created in step 11. The location of this crease isn't critical, so experiment with various widths for the undercarriage of the Zoomerang. Unfold these pre-creases.

15 Finally valley fold up the remaining wing, to lie upon the other to complete the Zoomerang.

13 Carefully refold step 10, the large flaps folding outward on existing creases.

HOW TO USE

The finished model will have a thin strip running down the length of the undercarriage. Take hold of this section, fairly close to the front of the Zoomerang. Hold the Zoomerang straight out in front of you, perpendicular to the ground, and with the nose uppermost, as shown. Raise your arm quickly, launching the model into the air. You can expect it to loop-the-loop, and return. You may need to make certain adjustments to the wings, and try different angles within the folding sequence, to achieve the desired results.
Keep practising.

14 Pinching the vertical centre line as a mountain fold, slide away from you and lie this folded edge on to the crease line made in step 12.

tumblewing

Kosho Uchiyama has designed this variation on a popular theme: a model which can be held high in the air, then dropped, causing it to spin as it comes to land. Use a square of thin, crisp paper, as there are quite a few layers building up in the design as you progress through the latter stages.

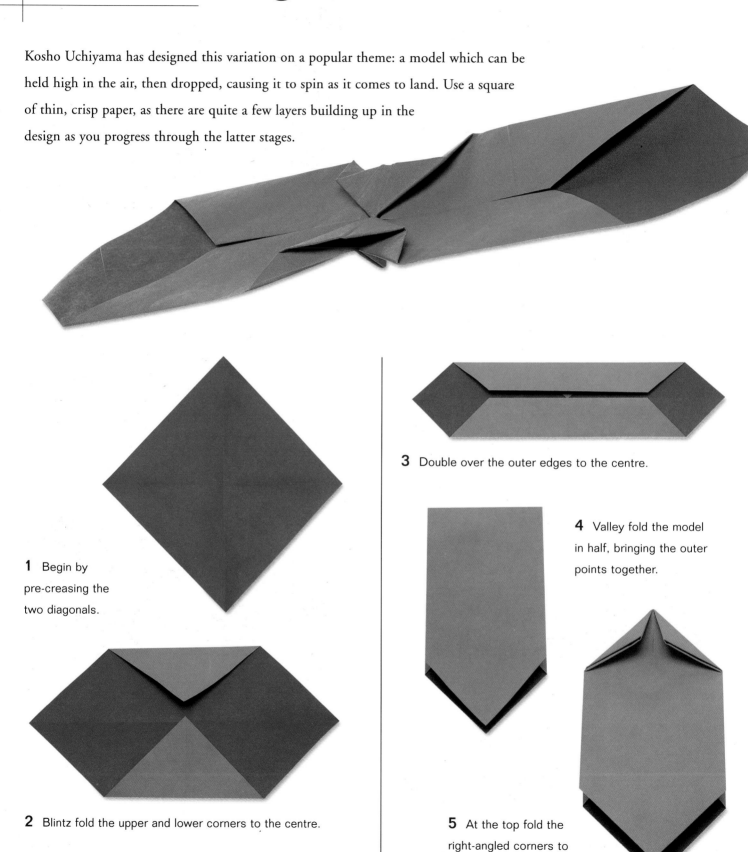

1 Begin by pre-creasing the two diagonals.

2 Blintz fold the upper and lower corners to the centre.

3 Double over the outer edges to the centre.

4 Valley fold the model in half, bringing the outer points together.

5 At the top fold the right-angled corners to the centre crease.

6 Unfold step 5, then inside reverse fold these corners into the model.

7 Fold the top corner (the closed point formed by the reverse folds previously made) down, to arrive at a point level with the two upper angles.

8 Leaving the small corner from step 7 firmly folded, open out the central valley fold once more, so that once again you have a long strip. The central area will not lie flat.

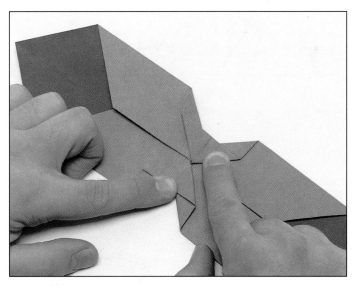

9 Squash the central flaps down symmetrically, forming a kind of bow-tie shape, to complete the Tumblewing.

HOW TO USE

Turn the model over, and raise the small triangular flap so that it projects upward at right angles to the rest of the model. Hold this point between your first two fingers, and then raise your arm high in the air, at approximately a 45° angle. Allow the model to slip from your fingers, and watch the effect as it gently spins away from you to the floor.

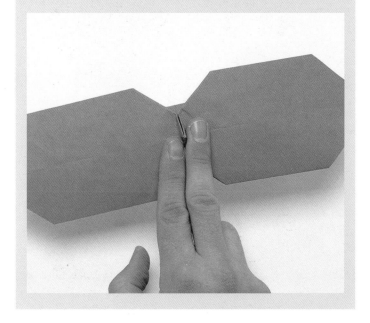

nodding dog

Paul Jackson devised this simple origami version of the classic car rear-window toy. As ever, it is important to fold with good, accurate creases, particularly as the action depends upon the sharpness of the folding. Use two squares of similarly coloured paper, preferably with a reverse colour. Begin by making the body, having the colour you wish to be predominant when you have finished the model face down.

1 For the body, fold and unfold the paper in half diagonally in both directions. Blintz fold all four corners to the centre.

2 Fold the model in half diagonally.

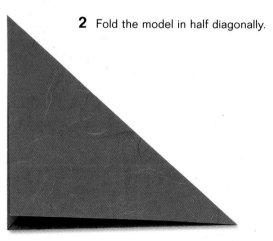

3 Fold the right point over to the left, keeping the lower edge level with itself. You might fold the point to meet with the base of the vertical crease line showing through the paper. This forms a simple tail.

4 Stand the completed body up.

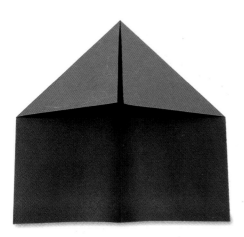

5 To make the head begin with the paper as a square, that is with horizontals and verticals, predominant colour face down, and fold in half side to side to fold in the vertical centre crease. Then fold the upper corners down to lie on the centre line.

6 Fold each of the triangular flaps upward and outward, so that the horizontal edges come to lie along the sloping edges.

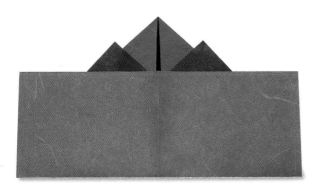

7 The two triangular flaps created in step 2 meet along the vertical centre line. Fold up the lower edge to a point a few millimetres/⅟₁₆–¼in above where they meet. This will form the eyes.

8 Fold the top point down to form the nose. The fold is about a third of the distance from the tip to the long horizontal edge.

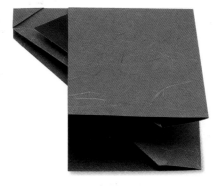

9 Mountain fold the model in half along the vertical centre line, so that the eyes remain on the outside.

HOW TO USE

Balance the head onto the sharp point at the top of the body. This point should go right up the centre of the head, and not caught in the side flaps. Gently push down on the nose with one finger, and the head will nod up and down.

magic star/frisbee

For this classic Bob Neale model, you will need eight small squares of paper, preferably smooth to the touch (rough, textured paper will spoil the easy action of the model).
Repeat all steps on each sheet of paper.

1 Fold the paper, in half side to side, pattern-/colour-side face down.

2 With the fold made in step 1 towards you, fold the lower right-hand corner up at 45° so that it lies along the upper raw edges, and makes a sharp point at the right-hand side.

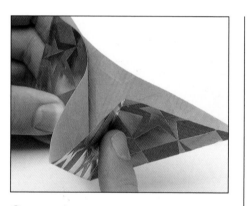

3 Open out step 2, and inside reverse fold this section of the paper.

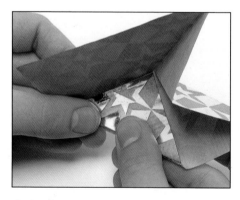

4 Open out the model slightly from above. At the other end, fold the remaining corners inside on 45° creases, to meet the folded edge. Collapse the paper flat once more.

5 Place the original unit on a table lying vertically. Make seven more units and arrange them on a table as shown.

6 Take any second unit, and slide it into position within the original unit, as shown, the second unit sliding between the open points of the first. Hold it in place.

7 Lock the units together by folding both of the excess tips of the open points of the first unit tightly over the edges of the second (the facing flap is mountain-folded, the rear flap valley-folded, as you look).

8 The first two units joined together.

9 Continue joining the remaining units clockwise. As shown, when you have joined six units, you seem to come to a point where you can go no further, and the ring looks almost complete. At this point you must carefully arrange the final two units so that, as you join them in sequence, you are also allowing unit one to be joined to unit eight.

HOW TO USE

The Magic Star completed. To convert to the Frisbee, take hold of any two opposite segments of the central octagon shape...,

... and gently slide outward, so that a hole begins to appear at the centre.

Then take hold of two different segments, and again slide outward, so that the hole opens up even more.

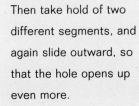

Keep rotating and repeating this process, until you have your Frisbee. To return to the Magic Star, simply repeat the opening process in reverse.

pecking crow

Some models contain a clever little move in the folding sequence that makes the design memorable. So it is with this action toy created by Makoto Yamaguchi, where folds are made through two layers of paper, so that when the layers are separated the folds are kept in place. Use a square of duo-coloured paper, with the predominant colour face down.

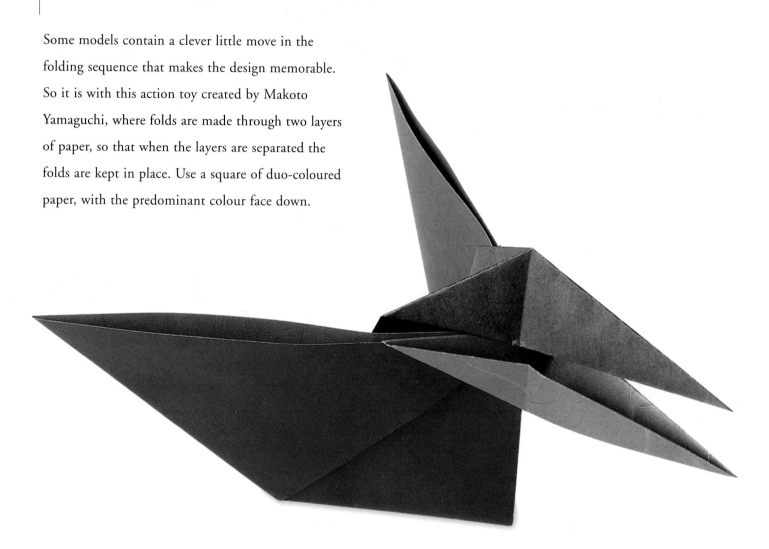

1 Begin by folding the paper in half diagonally. Then fold into quarters, merely to establish the vertical centre line as shown. Unfold.

2 Fold each of the double raw edges down to lie along the vertical centre crease.

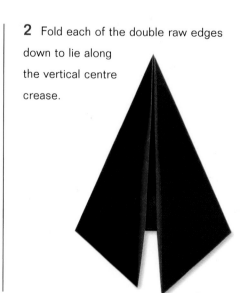

3 Fold each of the pointed flaps outward as far as they will go, so that the creases connect with the lower extreme corners. Their upper edges will be parallel to the lower horizontal edge.

4 Open out the section of paper at the top slightly, and you will observe one layer inside the other. Pull out the single upper layer, separating it from the outer layer wrapped around it.

5 Continue pulling the inner flap completely out.

6 Flatten the model.

7 Fold the upper corner (single layer only) down towards you as far as it will comfortably go.

8 Fold this point across to the right, so that the lower left edge comes up to lie along the central horizontal edge. Make a crease.

9 Unfold step 8, and repeat it in the other direction. Unfold once more.

10 Form a rabbit ear of the lower point, squeezing the paper together at the point, and allowing it to remain projecting upward at right angles to the rest of the model.

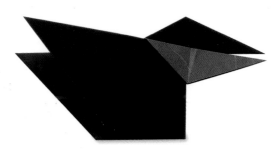

11 Turn the model over and repeat steps 7–10. Then mountain fold the model in half using the vertical centre crease. The completed Pecking Crow.

HOW TO USE

To make the beak open you pull the wings slightly apart.

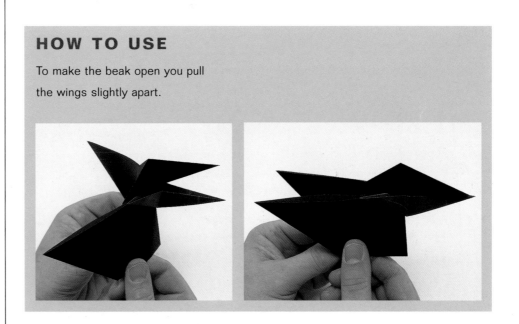

flapping bird

There are a great many flapping birds in origami, designed by folders worldwide, but my all-time favourite is this Paul Jackson variation on an original model by Sam Randlett. It has a wonderfully clean action that never fails to work; although there are a couple of moves that are quite tricky to understand. Use a square of crisp paper.

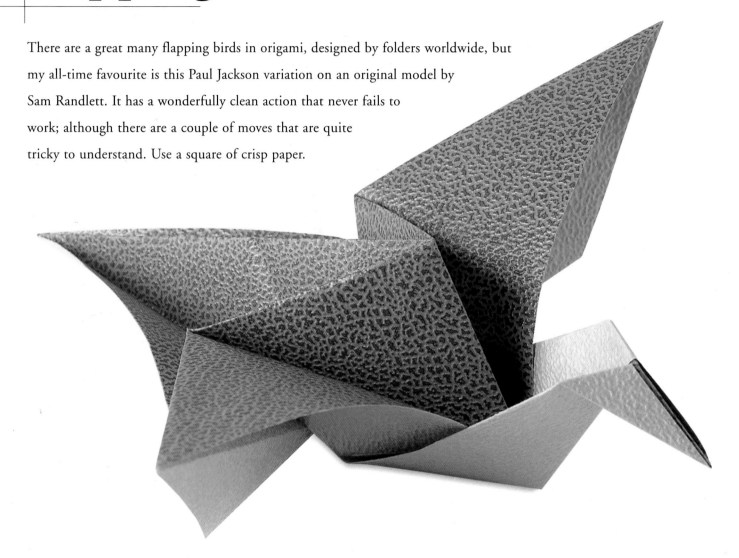

1 Begin with a Waterbomb base. The final model has a fairly equal colour ratio, so it never seems to matter which side of the paper faces you to begin with.

2 There are two sharp points on each side of the Waterbomb base. Fold the top point only on the right-hand side across to the left.

3 Fold the lower horizontal edge up to lie on the upper-right sloping edge. Make a really firm crease.

4 Unfold step 3.

5 Folding the single layer only, take hold of the uppermost point at the left, and make a repeat fold of step 3, using the same crease. As the flap comes to rest, you have to make a swivel-squash adjustment with excess paper between layers, so that the model will lie flat once more.

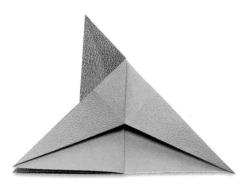

6 Step 5 completed.

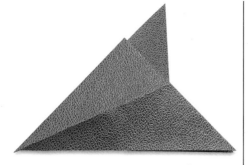

7 Turn the model over, and arrange it so that the crease made in step 3 rises from left to right.

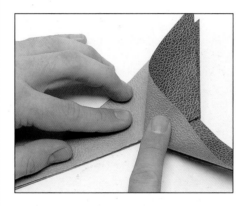

8 Repeat step 5 on this side, folding the single point at the right up to lie on the upper left sloping edge, matching the two wings together, and making a similar swivel-squash adjustment to that in step 5.

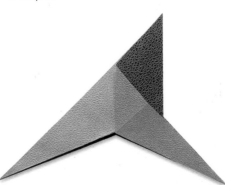

9 Step 8 completed.

10 Make a valley fold in the left-hand point, so that the crease runs in line with the lower edge of the right-hand point.

11 Change the angle of the left-hand point, by making another valley fold at the tip. These last two steps form the neck and head respectively.

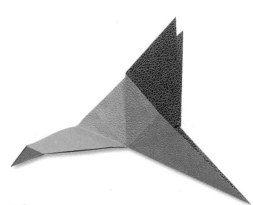

12 Open out steps 10–11.

▶

13 Turn the model over, so that you are now looking at the underside of the bird. Open out the pocket between the folded-edged layers of each of the sharp points, and hold with the point that has the creases made in steps 10–11 facing away from you.

14 Using the larger V shape of existing creases, outside reverse fold the neck into position. The point will be turned outside on itself.

15 Using the V shape of existing creases at the tip of the neck point, make a further outside reverse fold to form the head.

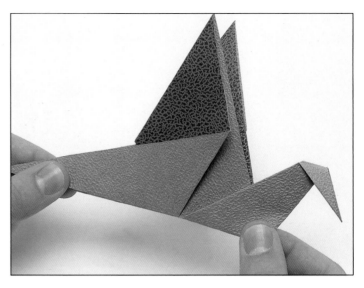

16 Flatten the model.

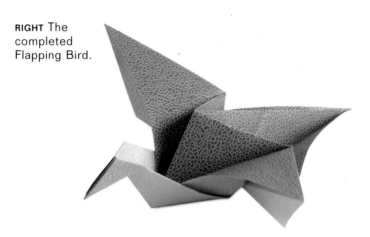

RIGHT The completed Flapping Bird.

HOW TO USE

Hold the chest of the bird with one hand, and the tail with the other. Pull the tail gently allowing the model to open slightly and collapse again, for a wonderful flapping action.

talking frog

Created by the folder Teruo Tsuji, this delightful model uses a common mechanism to produce a talking action. Use a large sheet (say, A3 [29 x 42cm/11½ x 16½in] cut square) of thin paper, as the layers do tend to become quite thick as you proceed through the folding sequence. Ideally, have green as the reverse colour, which should begin face down.

1 Fold the paper in half diagonally.

2 Fold the sharp points up to the top.

3 Fold in half diagonally again, this time only pinch-folding to find the centre of the model.

▶

4 Fold the sharp points down to the centre.

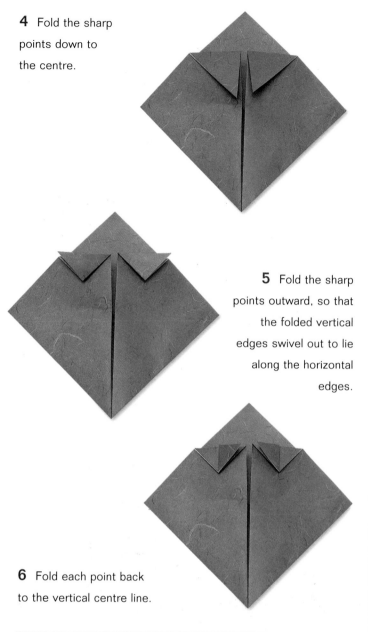

5 Fold the sharp points outward, so that the folded vertical edges swivel out to lie along the horizontal edges.

6 Fold each point back to the vertical centre line.

7 Raise points on the natural hinge creases, so that they are at right angles to the rest of the model. Squash fold each point, forming half-Preliminary bases.

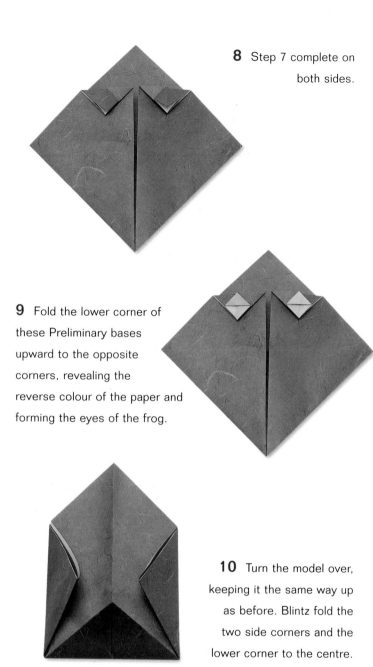

9 Fold the lower corner of these Preliminary bases upward to the opposite corners, revealing the reverse colour of the paper and forming the eyes of the frog.

10 Turn the model over, keeping it the same way up as before. Blintz fold the two side corners and the lower corner to the centre.

11 Make a rabbit ear of the lower blintzed flap, while folding the side corners back outward to their respective outside edges.

12 Carefully pinch-fold the upper portions of the model over the edges of the side flaps folded in step 11, creasing hard between the outer edges and the vertical centre line.

13 Step 12 completed on both sides.

14 Mountain fold the model in half, so that the two sides rest at approximate right angles with each other. While holding the model in this position with one hand, use the other hand to take hold of the single layer of paper at the top, and gently pull it downward, making a soft new crease, and forming a diamond shape in the frog's mouth.

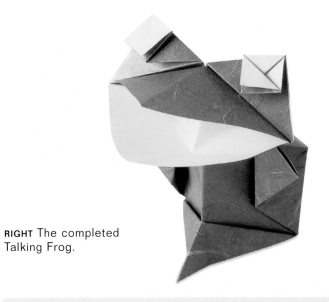

RIGHT The completed Talking Frog.

HOW TO USE

Allow the paper to relax for the mouth to open. Flex the vertical mountain crease, up the centre of the body back, to make the mouth close.

moving lizard

This design is perhaps one of the cleverest action toys, skilfully created by Tomoko Fuse. The locking mechanism of the units, which allows the various sections of the body to swivel and move, is really quite amazing. You will need 12 sheets of paper, all the same size, and preferably green on one side; begin with this side face down in every case.

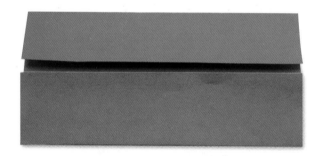

1 To make the legs, fold and unfold the first square in half, then fold the outer horizontal edges to the centre crease.

2 Turn the paper over.

3 At the right-hand edge, fold the outer corners inward to meet the centre line.

4 Unfold step 3.

5 Fold the right-hand edge across to the left, on a vertical crease, which connects the ends of the diagonal creases made in step 3.

6 The inner edge of the flap folded in step 5 is made from two layers of paper. Holding down the inner layer with one finger, pull the outer corner back to the right, squashing the paper to a point.

7 Repeat step 6 with the lower half.

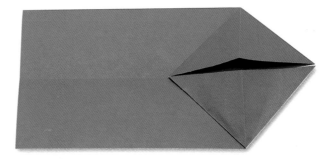

8 Steps 6–7 completed.

9 Fold the inner corner of this squashed diamond shape back out to the right, along the existing hinge crease.

10 Valley fold the model in half along the long centre crease, bringing the top half down to rest on the lower section. The completed leg. Make three more legs in the same way.

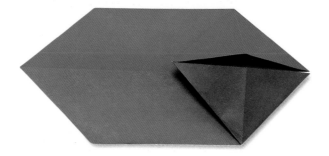

11 To make the head, begin at step 8 of the leg. Mountain fold the outer corners at the left underneath.

▶

12 To make the body, begin at step 8 of the leg, then repeat steps 3–8 at the left end of the model. Make three body sections.

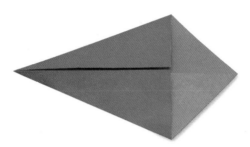

13 To make the tail, fold a kite base from another square, beginning with the green side face down.

14 Narrow the model by folding the outer long edges to the centre line.

15 Fold another square up to step 8 of the leg, then turn this unit over. Fold the corners at the left-hand edge inward to the centre crease. Make a really sharp crease.

16 Unfold step 15, then insert the wider end of the tail section into the open-ended portion of this section.

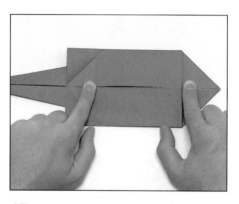

17 Keep pushing the tail piece inward, until the tip reaches the vertical crease (where the right hand is indicating in the photograph).

18 Pinching the upper crease made in step 15 as a mountain fold, swivel the loose corner down, and, pulling the excess paper tightly over the tail piece, squash the paper flat into its new position.

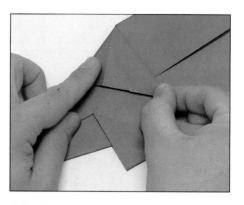

19 Step 18 in progress.

20 Step 18 completed. Note how there is now a tiny point projecting to the right of the vertical halfway line.

21 Mountain fold the tip of this point inside, tucking it under the central raw edge.

22 Repeat steps 18–21 on the other half of the model.

23 Turn the tail section over.

24 Take another sheet of paper, and, beginning with the green side face down, pre-crease in the vertical and horizontal halfway crease lines.

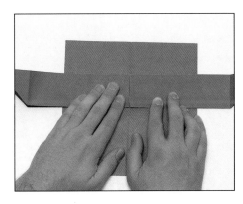

25 Lay one pair of legs in the position shown, where the lower edges run along the horizontal centre crease of the flat sheet of paper, and where the two legs meet in the middle.

26 Fold the upper corners down as far as they will comfortably go, the creases connecting the centre of the upper edge with the top edges of the legs.

27 Fold the lower edge of paper upward on the existing halfway crease, wrapping the paper tightly over the two legs.

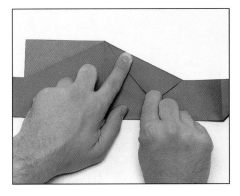

28 Holding the assembly together, carefully turn the model over. Repeat step 26 on the upper corners.

29 Make soft folds to the "thighs" of the lizard, by making diagonal creases, bringing lower edges to a vertical position, as shown. Turn the leg assembly over. Make another such assembly using the final sheet of paper, and the two other legs.

▶

30 To join the head, body and tail section take the head section and one body section in either hand. Twisting one around slightly as you push them together, allow the slit in the end of one unit to slide between and into the slit in the end of the other, then twist to flatten out.

31 Step 30 in progress.

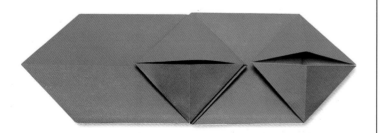

32 Step 30 completed.

33 Fold the opposite loose points of the central diamond section inward to lie along the vertical centre line, so that the two flaps lie together, as shown.

34 Tuck the tips of these two flaps under the central horizontal raw edges, locking this side of the model.

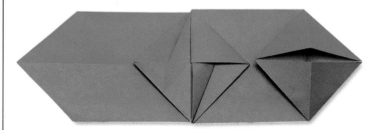

35 Lock from step 34 completed.

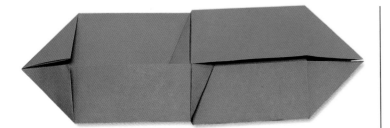

36 Turn the model over, and repeat steps 33–34 with the remaining points, to complete the lock on both sides.

37 The two locked units can move freely.

38 Assemble two more body units, and the tail section, as shown, in the same way as in steps 30–36.

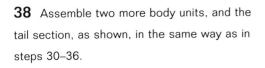

39 Slide the front leg assembly between the flaps of the two central diamond shapes of the body section nearest the head.

40 Step 39 in progress.

41 Finally slide the hind legs between similar flaps nearest the tail. The completed Moving Lizard.

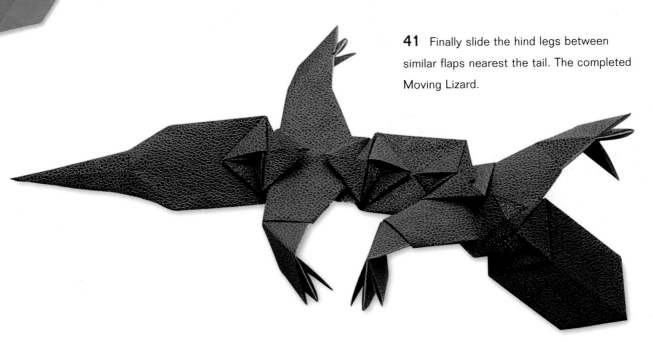

laughter lines

This simple trick can be done with any banknote bearing a portrait, or, failing that, you can quite easily devise the same principle by drawing a "smiley" face on a sheet of paper, except leave the mouth a straight horizontal line. The creases will then go vertically through each eye, and be close to the corners of the mouth.

1 Mountain fold the right hand edge of the note behind, making a sharp crease. If you are using a UK note this should go through one of the Queen's eyes.

2 Unfold completely, and repeat step 1 using the Queen's other eye.

3 Arrange the two existing creases at right angles, so that you appear to have the end of a box.

4 Push the end (showing the centre of the Queen's face) inward, and squeeze the paper flat, allowing a valley fold to form between the two existing mountain folds.

5 Open out the note, but do not pull flat; allow the V-shaped groove to remain in the paper. Now, if you look at the Queen's face straight on, she doesn't have much of an expression at all.

6 Twist the note so that the upper edge moves away from you, while the lower edge moves closer. Now look, the Queen has a smile.

7 If you now twist the note the other way, so that the upper edge moves closer while the lower edge moves further away, you will see a very miserable monarch indeed. The completed Laughter Lines.

fortune teller

This has to be the one model that virtually everyone remembers making as a child at school. It works like this: write four different colours on the outer petals of the completed model, number the eight panels on the inside, and underneath each panel write a "fortune". Ask a friend to name a colour, and then open and close the teller according to the number of letters that spell the chosen colour. The friend then chooses one of the visible numbers, and the teller is then opened and closed this number of times. The process is repeated, and, finally, the innermost flap is lifted to reveal the fortune.

1 Blintz fold the corners of a square. Turn the paper over and Blintz fold again.

2 Fold the model in half, bottom to top, then hold it as shown, and collapse Preliminary-base-style, using existing creases.

3 Step 2 completed.

4 Pull open the raw blintzed flaps folded in step 1.

5 Place fingers and thumbs into the four respective pockets created in step 4. The Fortune Teller can be flexed by first separating your two fingers from your two thumbs, and then separating your two hands, while pinching with each.

6 The secondary blintzed flaps folded at the end of step 1 are lifted up to reveal the fortune.

dollar shirt

This is an impressive traditional fold that is always popular at parties. You can ask to "borrow" a banknote from one of your audience and promise to show the owner a Gambler's Fold. At the conclusion, you can assure him that he need not worry about losing his money as he can "bet his shirt that he will get his money back". This can also be made using duo paper, as used here.

1 The illustration shows the model folded from a 2:1 (half a square) sheet of paper. The colour you begin with on top will form the collar and cuffs. If folding from most currencies of bank note, you will be able to make a fairly well-proportioned model from the note as it is. If folding from a US dollar, it is wise to make an extra fold to begin with, to change the proportions of the note: on the portrait face, fold one short side inward, to meet with the outside edge of the circular "frame". Then treat the note in the same way as any other. After folding and unfolding the paper in half, bringing the two longest sides together, fold these edges inward to the centre crease, then arrange the paper as shown.

2 Unfold step 1 and turn the paper over.

3 At the right, fold a thin strip, about 5mm–1cm (¼–½in) in width, revealing the colour for the collar.

4 Turn the paper over, and refold the long sides into the centre.

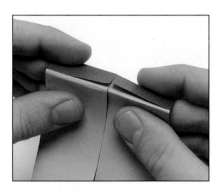

5 At the right-hand end, fold the reverse coloured strip behind, on a crease that runs along the edge, so that you are doubling the paper over by the same amount again.

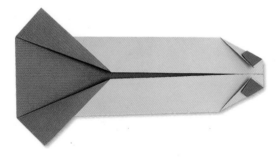

6 Fold the right-hand corners inward to meet the horizontal centre line. The corners rest at a point a short distance in from the right-hand edge, making creases which meet the outer edges at a fairly obtuse angle, as shown. This forms the collar. At the left-hand end of the model, fold the inner flaps outward, as far as they will comfortably go, that is to the extreme lower and upper corners. The angle of the fold is not critical, but you should have a small triangle projecting above and below the model. These folds will form the sleeves.

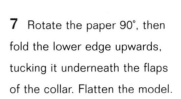

7 Rotate the paper 90°, then fold the lower edge upwards, tucking it underneath the flaps of the collar. Flatten the model.

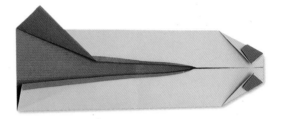

8 If you wish to add cuffs to the sleeves, unfold the model back to step 6, then also unfold the flaps that make the sleeves. Fold the long inner edges evenly outward, folding a very thin strip, from the open edge up to or slightly beyond the centre of the model. Do not worry if these two folds do not run level or meet, as this section of the paper will be hidden away on the final model. Then refold the sleeve flaps outward on existing creases. The photograph shows the lower flap with the necessary fold for the cuff. The upper flap shows the sleeve fold completed.

9 Finally, refold step 7 to complete the dollar shirt with cuffs.

envelope trick

Ed Sullivan designed a very clever model called an Un-unfoldable Box, which, as the name implies, was, once folded, impossible to unfold without tearing the paper. The principle used in this model lends itself to this trick with an ordinary envelope. Use a fairly stiff manilla office envelope, say A4 (21 x 29cm/8¼ x 11½in) in size.

1 For this trick, you trim the sealing flap from an envelope, and cut the top down by 1–2cm/½–1in, leaving raw edges. Then, using the following folding technique, secretly fold the raw edges completely outside on themselves. The idea of the trick is to show your friend the envelope so that he or she can see the folded edge, then you cut off the fold, leaving raw edges once again, and invite your friend to fold it again. Of course he or she will not be able to do so without tearing the paper and getting into a mess.

2 You now demonstrate how the trick is done. Fold the open end (both edges folded as one) over by 2–3cm/¾–1¼in.

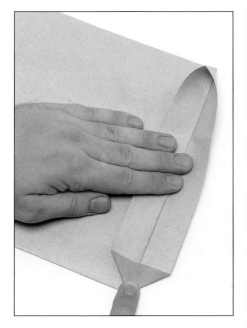

3 Unfold just the single upper layer folded in step 2, causing you to make two small triangular squash folds at each outer corner of the envelope.

4 Turn the envelope over.

5 Fold the two long outer edges inward, along the edges of the squash folds made in step 3.

6 Turn the model over, and mountain-fold the remaining outer edge of the envelope behind, as far as it will comfortably go. Now, each edge at the opening has been folded down, one either side.

7 Carefully place your fingers inside the opening of the envelope, and hold one corner between fingers and thumbs.

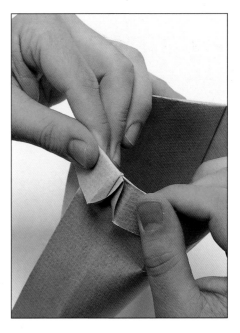

8 With extreme care, pull your hands apart, allowing the paper at the corner to stretch, and the excess hidden paper to be pulled free. Pull very slowly, until all the trapped paper is released.

9 Step 8 completed. Repeat at the other corner of the envelope. You will now have the same result as illustrated earlier: the end of the envelope will have been completely turned outside on itself.

blinking eyes

This cheeky action model was created by Jeremy Shafer. There are many variations on the same theme, with the same mechanism creating a mouth as well, and including four neighbouring heads out of one sheet of paper, making a barbershop quartet. The predominant colour for the final model should begin face down. Use a square of fairly thin, crisp paper.

1 Pre-crease the halfway horizontal centre line, and the vertical halfway centre line. Fold and unfold each time.

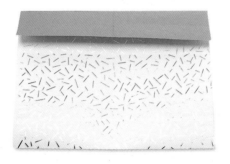

2 Fold the upper edge down to meet the horizontal crease.

3 Fold the lower edge about 3mm/⅛in higher than the halfway crease, then allow this flap to tuck underneath the first.

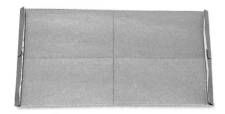

4 Turn the paper over. Fold in a thin strip of paper, about 3mm/⅛in, at each of the shortest sides.

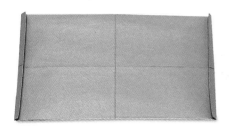

5 Double over once more the strips folded in step 4.

6 Turn the model over and fold the outer edges to the centre.

7 Collapse the model, mountain folding along the vertical centre crease.

8 Turn the model over. Opening out one half of the model slightly, reach inside and pull the upper raw edge out towards you, causing an inside reverse fold to be incorporated into this section, as you refold the paper flat. Allow the paper to be pulled out as far as it can go.

9 Step 8 in progress: shaping the upper eyelid.

10 Repeat with the other half.

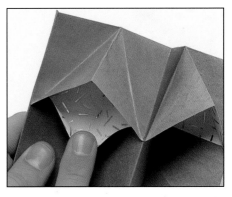

11 Repeat steps 8–10 with the remaining raw edges, forming the lower eyelids.

12 Hold the model at either end. If you allow the paper to collapse naturally, the eyes will appear open.

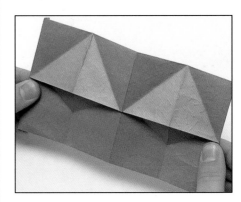

13 If you pull the ends fairly taut, the eyes will appear closed. Move your hands inward, then outward, to create the Blinking Eyes.

strawberry

This design by Rae Cooker makes an admirable alternative to the well-known traditional waterbomb. It is fun to fold as a party trick because there is a surprise finale as you inflate the model. If you are fortunate enough to find some giftwrap with red on one side and green on the reverse, this will be ideal.

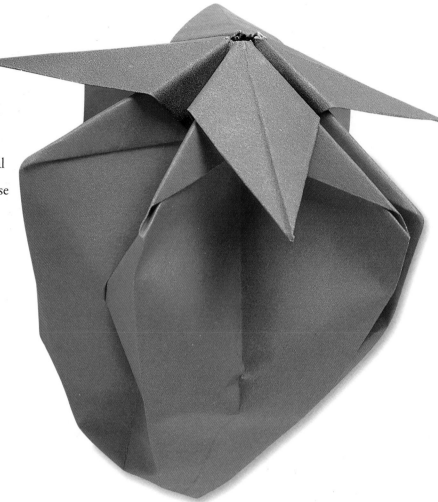

1 Beginning from a red-coloured Preliminary base, squash all the four large flaps into step 6 of the Frog base.

2 Using the vertical hinge crease as an axis, fold one of the large flaps at the right across to the left, to reveal a plain-coloured face.

3 Fold each of the lower sloping edges, single layer only, inward to lie along the vertical centre crease.

4 Fold the lower corner, single layer only, upward as far as it will comfortably go.

5 Repeat steps 3–4 on the remaining three plain faces. You will need to repeat step 2 on the reverse face, then rotate the layers in turn to make this possible.

6 Step 5 completed. Rotate the layers once more so that you have a plain face on top.

7 Fold each of the lower short edges upward to lie along the vertical centre line. The crease extends to the outermost corners left and right.

8 Repeat step 7 on the three remaining similar faces.

9 There are eight large flaps in total, around the central axis. Separate them into pairs, causing the model to appear three-dimensional, and hold between fingers and thumbs in-between each pair of flaps. The grouping should be such that your fingers and thumbs lie upon the green points folded in steps 4–5.

10 Carefully use your fingers and thumbs to flip up all four of these reverse-coloured flaps (the stalk), so that they form a "propeller" at the top of the model.

11 Now take a deep breath, place your lips right up to the hole at the top of the model, and give a good sharp blow into the strawberry. It will magically inflate. If you blow too hard, you will end up with a tomato!

kissing lips

Designed by Soon Young Lee, this has to be one of my all-time favourite action models. You begin by making a series of folds, only to unfold everything back to the original square. You then refold all the existing creases in a new sequence to produce a final model of elegant simplicity yet delightfully comic working. Use a square of crisp paper, preferably red on one side. Begin with this side uppermost.

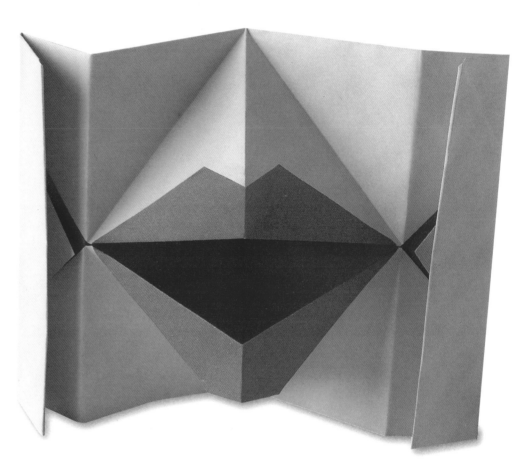

1 Fold the paper in half diagonally.

2 Fold the sharp point at the right over to the left, a third of the entire distance of the horizontal edge.

3 Fold the sharp point at the left over to the right in the same way.

4 Fold each point in turn to meet with the upper corners, as shown.

5 Now fold each point down to the lower corners, as shown.

6 Swivel the sloping edge of the small triangular flaps to lie along the folded edges made in step 5.

7 There will now be two tiny triangular points projecting out from the sides of the model. Fold these in half, folding the tips downward, as shown.

8 Open out every fold made thus far, and arrange so that the reverse colour is now uppermost, and all the creases are at the upper and lower corners of the paper.

9 Using the creases made in step 7, fold in the tips of each opposite corner.

10 Using the creases made in step 6, fold the two upper edges inward to form rabbit ears with each opposite corner.

11 Turn the paper over, and use existing creases formed in steps 2–3 to fold each opposite corner section in to the middle. The paper should not be forced to flatten here, but allowed to be left slightly three-dimensional, so that the two lips are not damaged.

12 Fold the whole model in half side to side, allowing the V shape of creases folded in step 4 to re-form. One of the creases in this V is currently a mountain, where both should be valley folds. Manually change the mountain to a valley on both lip sections, before making this collapse. ▶

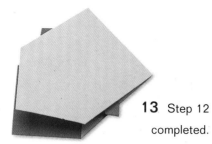

13 Step 12 completed.

RIGHT The completed kissing lips.

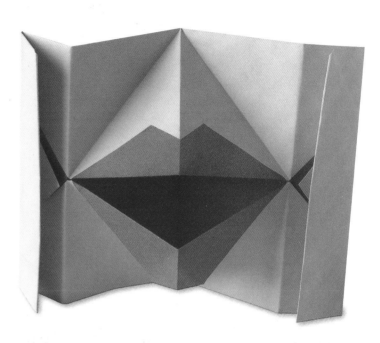

14 Fold the single upper layer away from you as far as it will comfortably go. The corners meet logically.

HOW TO USE

Repeat steps 14–16 on the reverse face. Hold the model between fingers and thumbs, by the two side panels made in step 16. This double-folded section needs to be raised to rest at 90° to the rest of the model.

15 To hide the colour of the large diamond shape, fold the raw corner back towards you, as shown.

Pull gently apart, so that the lips "kiss". With a little ingenuity, you can mount the lips inside the folded spine of a card, to produce a pop-up kiss card.

16 Double the folded edge created in step 15 over once more, creating a rectangular section. This is the area of paper held when working the model.

money pig

This design by Paul Jackson has been slightly simplified so that it can be made quickly. If the banknote isn't quite 2:1 in proportion (British £5 notes are the closest to it), then perhaps use a very fine fold or two down either edge to match this proportion. Here, the model is seen made from paper. Preferably use paper that is the same colour on both sides, as both sides of the paper show on the final model.

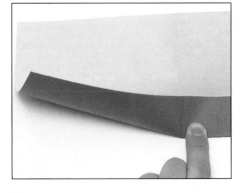

1 Pre-crease the vertical centre line by folding and unfolding the shortest sides together. Turn the paper over, so that the crease you have made appears now as a mountain fold. Arrange the paper so that the longest edges are horizontal.

2 Valley-fold the horizontal centre crease by folding and unfolding bottom to top. Then fold the lower long side to the horizontal centre crease, but only crease from the vertical centre line outward to the right side.

3 Unfold step 2, and repeat with the upper edge. Unfold the paper completely.

▶

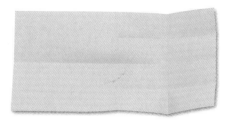

4 Fold the right edge across to the left, so that it lies along the vertical centre line. Unfold once more.

5 The paper is turned around here for clarity. Take hold of the vertical centre crease (the mountain fold) between fingers and thumbs, as shown. Slide the paper away from you, until you can bring the mountain-folded edge down to lie along the crease made in step 4. Flatten the model.

6 Step 5 completed.

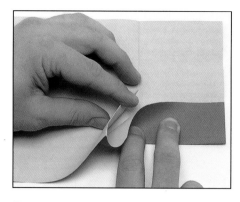

7 At the right-hand side, refold the outer edges into the horizontal centre line made in step 2. Beneath the pleat formed in steps 5–6, you will need to make a 45° diagonal fold across the underside of the pleated section.

8 Step 7 completed.

9 Turn the paper over, but keep it arranged in the same way. Fold the square at the left in half diagonally, bringing the lower edge to lie along the vertical edge. Crease only between the lower right corner of this square and the centre. Unfold.

10 Repeat step 9 folding the upper edge to the vertical edge, creasing in the same way, and unfolding.

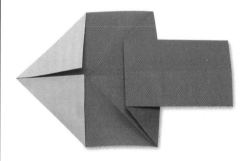

11 Fold the two left corners inward to lie along the horizontal centre crease.

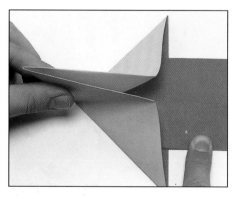

12 Using the two creases made in steps 9–10, and the left-hand half of the horizontal centre crease, pinch the left corner to a point, forming a kind of rabbit ear.

13 Allowing the rabbit ear fold in step 12 to open out slightly, lift the section of paper from beneath (the pleated portion), and let it rest on top of the raised point.

14 Valley fold the model in half along the horizontal centre crease, and, as you do so, push the section of paper released in step 13 in-between the layers of the raised point. This will lock the model together well, and help prevent the legs splaying apart.

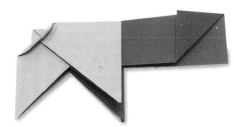

15 Suggest the pig's tail by making a valley/mountain pleat in the upper left corner. At the right, fold the short vertical edge upward, single layer only, to lie along the upper edge.

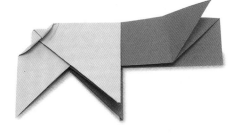

16 Unfold the lower right corner, then inside reverse fold it.

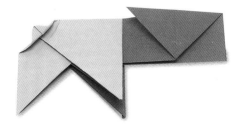

17 Swing the point created by step 16 across to the left.

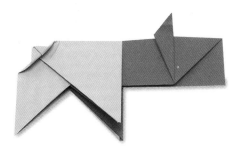

18 Fold the sloping edge of this point upward to a vertical position. This is the ear.

19 Repeat steps 15–18 on the reverse face of the head. Make two inside reverse folds at the front of the head, first of all reversing the point inside the head, then with another reverse fold closer to the point, reverse the paper back out again, to suggest the snout. Turn the tip of the snout outside on itself; you will need to open the point up slightly from below to be able to do this.

20 Holding the body between finger and thumb of one hand, take hold of the head with the other, and crimp fold the head down slightly.

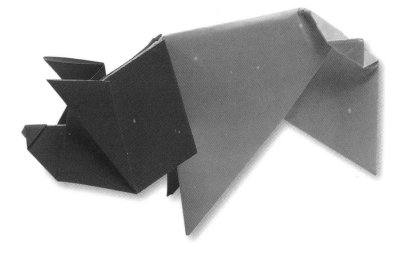

LEFT The completed Money Pig.

spinner

One of many wonderful designs by the late Lewis Simon, this model combines two standard bases, the Waterbomb base and the Preliminary base, to form a rigid modular construction. Use 12 sheets of fairly sturdy paper. The outer colour of the entire model will be the same as the outer colour of the Preliminary bases.

1 Fold six Waterbomb and six Preliminary bases. Open out one of each base slightly, and allow the Preliminary base to wrap around the outside of the Waterbomb base, lining up the creases in the two bases.

2 Mountain fold each of the four corners of the Preliminary base inward, over the outer raw edges of the Water-bomb base, locking the sheets of paper together.

3 Allow the Waterbomb base to reform, the two sheets folded as one. Repeat for the remaining bases.

4 Join any two units together by slipping the raw (Waterbomb) point of the first unit over the raw point of the other, but underneath the raw edge created by the Preliminary base. Push in all the way, until the two edges of what were the Preliminary bases meet.

5 In the same way, join adjacent points of the first two units into similar points of a third unit, forming a triangular section in the centre, as shown.

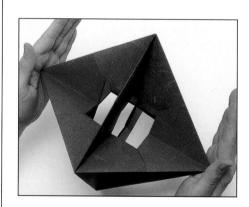

6 Add the final units in the same way; the last unit is the most difficult to add. To activate the model place the points of the completed spinner into the centre of your open palms, holding firmly. Blow hard against the top point of the model, and the spinner will really spin.

butterfly ball

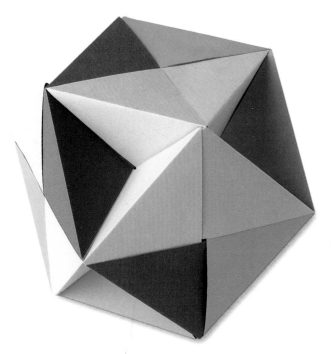

This apparently solid geometric shape, designed by Kenneth Kawamura, can be hit open-handed in mid-air, where it explodes, cascading colourful butterflies everywhere. A shallow square box can be used to help support the sides of the Butterfly Ball while you add more units. Use 12 squares of fairly heavyweight paper.

1 Fold a Waterbomb base then pull open the front and rear faces. The angle along the lower edge (inside the model), where adjacent points meet, should be a right angle. Make 11 more units.

2 Place a unit, triangle side down, on to your folding surface. Place a second unit inside the first at 90° to it so that half of the triangle overlaps. Connect with two more units so that the triangular faces form an interwoven pattern at the base.

3 Each side of the Butterfly Ball will appear the same, so, when adding the next tier of units, turn each of the four waterbomb bases around, so that the points are projecting upwards and downwards. As you slot each unit into place at the corners, make sure that once again you interweave the points over and under, so that the model will hold together at the end. In each lower corner inside the ball, there is a triangular construction of three units; make sure that each one lies both over and under its neighbour.

4 The second tier of units all added.

5 Add the third and final tier of units in the same way. You will complete a four-unit weave on top in just the same way as you started at the base. Have patience as you add the last 2–3 units. The completed Butterfly Ball. To burst the model: throw it gently into the air. As it descends, use the palm of your hand to smack the ball back upward. The ball will open in a spray of colour, as the butterflies shower to the ground.

Japanese brocade

This design, by Minako Ishibashi, makes attractive earrings, when folded from extremely small squares, say 4 x 4cm/1½ x 1½in. For a practice version, begin with six squares of fairly sturdy paper. This modular design is very original, featuring curved surfaces, which seem to create the illusion of rings encircling the central cube shape. Only one colour shows on the finished unit, so begin with this colour face down. Two squares each of three different colours can also be used, as here.

1 Begin by folding the square in half in one direction, to establish the centre line. Fold upper and lower edges in to meet this crease.

2 Fold the right vertical edge upward on a diagonal crease to lie along the upper edge. Fold the left vertical edge downward to lie on the lower edge. This forms a parallelogram.

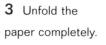

3 Unfold the paper completely.

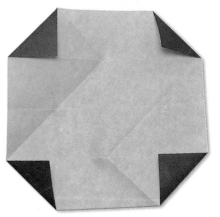

4 Fold all four corners inward to lie on the horizontal quarter creases. Two of these creases will already have been made.

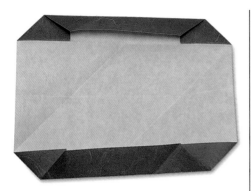

5 Fold the upper and lower edges in to lie along the horizontal quarter creases.

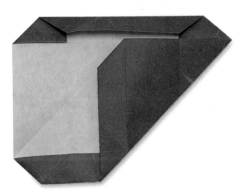

6 Fold the lower right flap inward on the existing crease, made in step 2.

7 Peel back the inner vertical edge of the flap folded in step 6, on an existing parallel crease, while at the same time folding up the lower edge, also on the existing crease. This performs both a swivel and a squash fold.

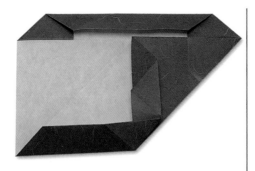

8 Step 7 completed.

9 Repeat steps 6–7 for the top left flap.

10 Pull out the lower border, and allow the flap folded in step 9 to tuck in behind it. Flatten the model once more.

11 Step 10 completed.

12 Turn the model over, and fold each of the sharp points to the obtuse angles of the parallelogram, as shown.

13 Allow the flaps folded in step 12 to be unfolded slightly, to rest at right angles to the central square shape. Make five more identical units.

▶

14 To assemble, slide the point of any one unit under the central section of another unit, as shown.

15 Continue by adding a third unit, assembling the central cube piece by piece. If folding with two units of three different colours, you should add units of the same colour opposite each other. All the units are joined in the same way, all the way around the model.

16 Under construction.

17 Assembly finished.

18 Finally, squeeze together the four flaps that appear on each of the six faces of the central cube, allowing them to project upward slightly and form the circular "bands" around the model.

RIGHT The completed Japanese Brocade.

five intersecting tetrahedra

This ingenious design was devised by Tom Hull, using a unit created by Francis Ow. The original form was a simple tetrahedron: a skeletal frame made from six individual struts. Tom found a way of interweaving five tetrahedra to create the final masterpiece shown. This is a highly complex model to assemble, and it is important to understand just how the units are interwoven. To assist you, the final steps show stages of two tetrahedra, three tetrahedra, four tetrahedra and finally the intersecting five modular constructions. Use ten squares of fairly stiff paper, ideally two sheets of five different colours. Divide each square into thirds by folding, then trim down the fold lines, yielding three 1 : 3 strips. You will eventually have 30 strips of paper, ready to fold the model. This model can also be made from US dollar notes.

1 Begin with the strip positioned horizontally lengthways. The colour on top to begin with will not show on the final model. Fold the paper in half, bringing the two longest sides together, to establish the horizontal centre crease. Unfold. Then fold upper and lower edges to the centre line.

2 Pick up the model from your folding surface. At the far end, fold the right folded edge into the centre, but pinch-crease only, creasing 3–4cm/1¼ x 1½in down from the short upper edge.

3 Fold the upper left-hand corner across to the right, so that it comes to rest upon the pinch-crease made in step 2. The crease you are now making also connects with the centre of the short upper edge.

4 Fold the upper right-hand corner over the edge of the small triangle created in step 3, which will make the two sides equal in the angle, and amount of corner folded.

5 Open out step 4.

6 Open out step 3 (the left corner) and begin to inside reverse fold the corner inwards on existing creases. This step shows the move in progress.

7 Step 6 completed.

8 At the right corner, fold the upper horizontal edge down to meet the crease made in step 4.

9 Using the crease made in step 4, double over the outer edge at the right.

10 Repeat steps 2–10 at the other end of the strip. Once again, begin by pinch-creasing the right side, so that the little inside reverse folds are formed at opposite corners.

11 Fold the strip in half along its length, then allow to open out slightly, the correct resting angle becoming clearer when you begin the assembly. Allow the tiny triangular flaps at top right to open out slightly, as these are the locking tabs. The completed unit. Fold another 29.

12 Turn each unit over, so that as you lock them together, you are looking at the outside (the smooth face) of the paper. Lock any two units by carefully sliding the small triangular tab on one unit into the slit pocket (the inside reverse fold made in steps 6–7) of the other.

13 Step 12 completed. See how the units fit flush together, so that they sit at the correct angle to which further units can be joined.

14 In the same way, join a third unit to the second unit, then the first unit to the third, to produce a point consisting of the sides of all three units.

15 Add three more units of the same colour, to form the single tetrahedron.

16 The finished tetrahedron from a slightly different angle, showing the construction. When adding further tetrahedra, you will need to leave some corners open until you have interwoven the separate constructions correctly. Only then can you make the locking connections.

17 Tom Hull's advice on how to add the completed tetrahedra is that there is a very strong symmetry behind the formation of this structure, and understanding this symmetry can aid you in the construction. The finished object should have the following property: any two tetrahedra are interwoven with one corner poking through a hole in the other, and vice versa, like a three-dimensional Star of David, but slightly twisted.

18 Three tetrahedra interwoven.

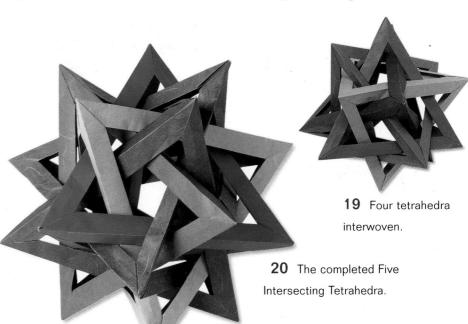

19 Four tetrahedra interwoven.

20 The completed Five Intersecting Tetrahedra.

modular star

One of the most prolific origami authors is the Japanese expert Tomoko Fuse, who is most famous for her decorative multi-piece boxes and modular stars. This star has long been a favourite, and you should find the assembly fairly straightforward. The units themselves, 30 in total, are also quite easy to realize. Use sturdy paper with the same colour both sides, as trying to work out an appropriate colour sequence with the final construction can be quite a challenge in itself. Furthermore, many people feel that this works better since it allows the modular piece to be seen as a whole; lots of bright colours can sometimes distract the eye from its simplicity and elegance.

1 Arrange the paper as a diamond shape, then fold and unfold the paper in half in both directions, bringing outer edges together. Pre-crease the vertical diagonal.

2 Fold the lower corner up so that it meets with the halfway fold currently running lower left edge to upper right edge. The crease you are going to make ends at the right corner. This is quite tricky, because the crease approaches the right corner at a very acute angle, so fold carefully.

3 You are now going to swivel and squash fold the paper. On the flap created in step 2, pinch the crease that was originally the diagonal into a mountain fold, swivelling the point across to lie on the vertical crease line beneath.

4 Step 3 in progress.

5 Step 3 completed. Repeat steps 3–4 on the upper corner. Flatten the model.

6 Fold the lower right sloping edge upward to lie along the vertical centre crease.

7 Running underneath the inner edge of the flap folded in step 6, there is a very narrow strip, which forms a pocket. Tuck the small triangular point created by the swivel in steps 3–4 into the pocket beneath this narrow edge.

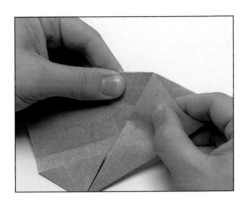

8 Carefully pull the flap folded in step 6 across to the right, just to make sure that it is locked in place, and is not allowed to slide.

9 Steps 7–8 completed. Repeat steps 6–8 with the neighbouring flap.

10 Turn the model over. Fold the second shortest side across to lie on the long side.

11 Repeat at the other end. The outline of the model should be a diamond shape.

12 Turn the model over, and fold in half, bringing the two sharp points together. Allow to unfold.

▶

13 Allow the flaps folded in steps 10-11 to open out slightly, completing the unit, which now appears three-dimensional. Make another 29 units in the same way.

14 Take any two units. Slide the point of one unit into the central slit in the diamond-shaped face of the other.

15 Two units assembled.

16 Assemble a three-unit cluster, by adding a third unit in the same way. You will now also need to connect the third unit to the first. This requires swivelling the construction into position to allow these locks to be performed.

BELOW The completed Modular Star.

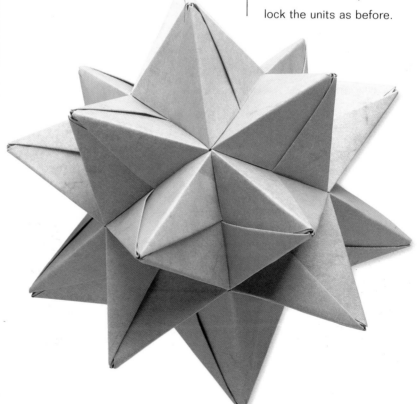

17 When more units are added, you will notice that a ring of any five points forms a pentagonal star, as shown.

18 Near to completion. Continue to lock the units as before.

modular cube

One of several variations along a similar theme, this 12-piece modular cube by Lewis Simon is a favourite. The units are very simple to fold, the construction slightly more challenging; you slot points into pockets, with the middle section of each unit making up the principal part of two adjacent sides, while the ends of each unit fold around right-angled corners to lock the model together. Ideally use duo paper, beginning with the same side facing upward each time.

1 Begin by dividing a square of paper into thirds horizontally.

2 Refold the lower third.

3 Fold the raw edge of the third folded in step 2 back down to the lower edge. ▶

4 Unfold step 3.

5 Fold the raw edge once more, this time halfway, to the crease made in step 3.

6 Double the folded edge created in step 5 over once more, giving an extra thickness to the long, thin horizontal strip.

7 Repeat steps 2–6 on the upper portion of the paper.

8 Using a diagonal crease, fold the right-hand vertical edge downward, to lie along the lower horizontal edge. At the left, fold the outer edge away from you to the upper edge. You will have a parallelogram.

9 Unfold step 8.

10 Refold step 8, allowing the triangular flap at the left to tuck in underneath the horizontal border strip on the upper portion of the paper.

11 Flatten the model.

12 Repeat steps 10–11 at the right.

13 Turn the model over.

14 Make folds at each end, so that the small, reverse-colour triangles are folded in half diagonally.

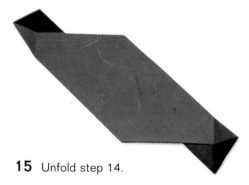

15 Unfold step 14.

16 Valley fold the model across the centre, bringing the shortest sides of the parallelogram together; the two obtuse angles will meet by this fold.

17 Partially open out step 16, so that there is a right angle between the two sides of the unit. Make a further 11 units.

18 Slot a second unit into the first, by the method shown: the end tab goes under the long, thin central border, pushes in until it folds around the angle to the adjacent side, and locks into place.

19 Step 18 in progress.

20 Add a third unit, locking by the same method. The tab on the third unit is then slotted into the "pocket" of the first unit, thus creating a triangular, truncated corner.

21 Step 20 completed.

22 Continue adding further units in the same way.

LEFT The completed Modular Cube is best displayed standing on one of the truncated corners.

kusudama

A kusudama is a decorative modular ball. You can either fold it from paper you prepare yourself, or from kits that you can buy, which also include instructions and a beautiful tassel and loop by which to hang your finished model. Here, 30 squares of paper are required. Unlike many modular designs, the assembly of the units is made by slotting points into pockets on the inside of the model. This makes it a very complicated model to assemble, and patience will be needed.

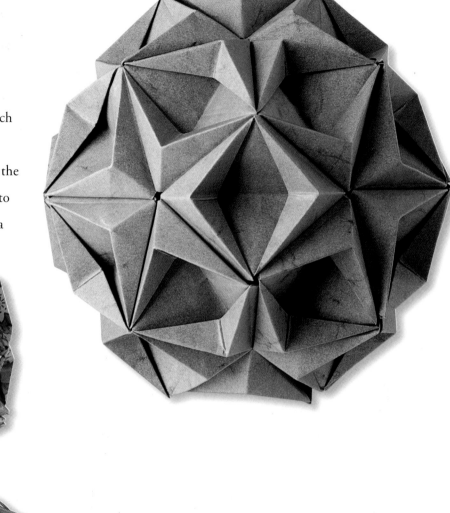

1 Begin by folding and unfolding your first square in half, to establish the horizontal centre crease. Fold upper and lower edges to the centre.

2 Using 45° diagonal folds, bring the right edge up to lie along the upper edge. Fold the left edge down to lie along the lower edge. This forms a parallelogram.

3 Unfold step 2, and turn the paper over. Note the position of the creases made in step 2. Pre-crease the vertical centre line by folding in half, side to side, and unfolding.

4 Repeat step 2 on this side.

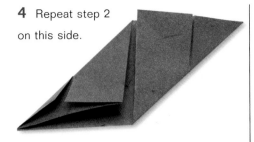

5 Unfold step 4.

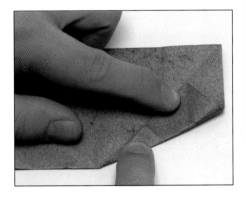

6 Fold the outer edges to the centre.

7 Unfold step 6. Fold the right half of the lower edge up to meet with the diagonal fold made in step 4. Pinch-crease only from the lower edge to halfway across the right-hand panel, so that the crease you are now making meets with the vertical crease made in step 6.

8 Unfold step 7, then bring the lower edge up to meet the diagonal crease on the right made in step 2 (now appearing as soft mountain folds). Again pinch-crease, this time from the lower right-hand corner to the vertical crease, which halves the right-hand section of the model. This pinch-crease, and the one made in step 7, will form a V shape.

9 As you refold the vertical crease made in step 6, allow this V shape to form an inside reverse fold, as you collapse the paper.

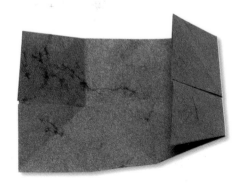

10 Step 9 completed.

11 Repeat steps 7–10 on the upper left section of the model. Turn the model 180° to do this. Allow the model to unfold as shown.

12 Refold the diagonal creases made in step 4.

13 Using a crease that lies beneath the central diamond shape, collapse the paper in half. The diamond will look like a mouth closing. Flatten the model to make good strong creases throughout, then allow to open up slightly.

▶

14 Firmly crease the fold line that cuts across the outer points, forming little triangular flaps at each end of the unit. The Unit complete. Make 29 more.

15 Turn the first unit over, so that you are looking at the reverse face. Take a second unit, and assemble as shown: the point of the second unit goes into the slit at the rear of the first unit.

16 Step 15 completed. Allow the form to remain three-dimensional.

17 Joining three units: take a third unit, and assemble as before, tucking the point into the slit at the rear of the second unit.

18 Now join the third unit to the first, forming a point on the underside, while a triangular cavity appears face up. You will have to swivel the units into the correct position to make this possible.

19 Steps 17–18 in progress.

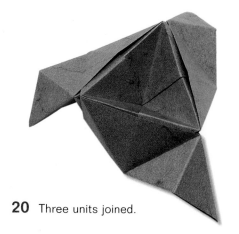

20 Three units joined.

21 Three units joined, the outside view.

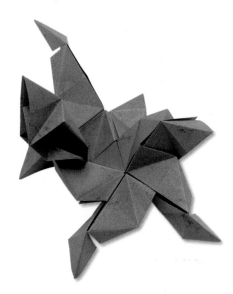

22 Keep adding further units as before. At this point it is helpful to look at the illustration of the final model: see how five of the "mouth" formations of the original unit circle around to form a pentagonal star shape.

23 The Star shape. This will be the outer face of the Kusudama. You may find it helpful to use a shallow box lid, approximately the size of the opening spread of ten or so units. The edges will support the side units as they are assembled, allowing the Kusudama to form into a three-dimensional shape without the weight of individual units pulling themselves and the others out of the locking position.

26 More units added. You can use a paper clip to hold units together while you add the final ones, if you like.

27 Adding the final units. You must make sure each pocket is ready to receive a point. It helps to hollow the pocket out with a sharp tool just prior to locking, and also make sure that the points are sharply folded, and lie at the right angle to simply slot in. This is a very complicated assembly procedure, so accept it as a challenge.

24 More units added.

BELOW The completed Kusudama.

25 More units added.

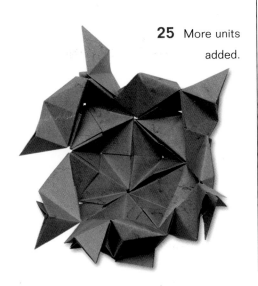

fireworks

There are many examples in origami of what we call Flexagons, often multi-piece, where the final model can rotate and flex, producing a kaleidoscope effect. This one, designed by Yami Yamauchi, was the highlight of the International Origami Convention held by OUSA (Origami USA) a few years ago. The units are very easy to make, the construction slightly more difficult, especially the last two units. Use 12 squares of fairly crisp, strong paper. This is an extremely enjoyable model to fold, and great fun to play around with when completed.

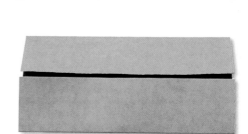

1 Begin with the first square arranged with horizontal and vertical outer edges. The colour showing predominantly on the final unit should be uppermost. Fold in half bottom to top, to pre-crease the horizontal centre line. Fold upper and lower edges to this crease line.

2 Unfold step 1, turn the paper over, then fold and unfold in half diagonally in both directions.

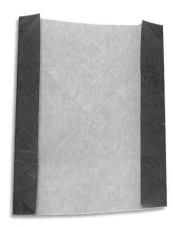

3 With the quarter creases remaining horizontal, as shown, fold the left and right edges inward to meet with the intersection of the outer quarter and diagonal pre-creases. Crease firmly here.

4 Unfold step 3, then form a Waterbomb base allowing the diagonals to fold naturally as valley creases.

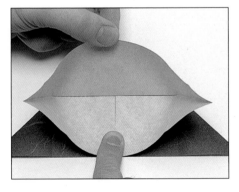

5 Lift up the lower edge, single layer only, so that it meets the upper point.

6 Then squash the flap into a kind of tent shape (the point of the Waterbomb base comes to rest at the centre of the lower edge).

7 Step 6 completed.

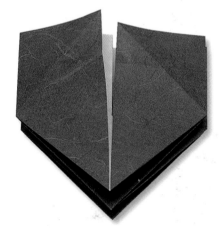

8 Repeat steps 5–7 on the reverse face, then rotate the paper 180° into the position shown.

9 Fold the upper raw edge, single layer only, down on the creases made in step 3. To be able to flatten the model, you will need to allow a small triangular-shaped squash fold to form at the upper corners.

10 Repeat on the adjacent flap, and on the reverse face.

11 Unfold steps 9–10. The completed unit. Fold 11 more.

▶

12 Each unit consists of four large flaps, two to the right, and two to the left of the model. There is also a slit down the vertical centre of each unit, with a pocket behind. The vertical centre crease can be used to fold the flaps over from one side of the model to the other. Opening out the two pockets on the first unit, slide in the rear flaps of the second unit.

13 This shows the right side being worked on.

14 The first two units together.

15 Fold one large flap at the left across to the right, using the vertical centre crease. Parts of both units will be folded across as one.

16 Refold the squash-fold arrangements made originally in steps 9–10.

17 Now turn the paper over, and fold two flaps across from right to left.

18 Repeat step 16.

19 Turn the layers so that once again everything is symmetrical, and there are an equal number of large flaps to the right and left. The upper layer will look something like a heart, as the upper corners of this unit will now be missing.

20 Continue adding more units in the same way.

21 All twelve units added. Now, to join the last unit to the first, very carefully swing both ends around into a ring. Even more carefully (so that the previously locked units do not come apart) tuck the units together, then make the necessary squash folds to complete the model.

RIGHT The completed Fireworks.

HOW TO USE

Hold carefully with each palm, so that your fingers are underneath, and the model is cupped in your hands. Hold firmly, and push up with your fingers from underneath. The central section will rise towards you, and Fireworks will be able to flex into a different form. This process can be repeated again and again.

index